Also by Stuart Stevens

The Innocent Have Nothing to Fear: A Novel

*The Last Season: A Father, a Son, and
a Lifetime of College Football*

*The Big Enchilada: Campaign Adventures with the Cockeyed
Optimists from Texas Who Won the Biggest Prize in Politics*

Feeding Frenzy: Across Europe in Search of the Perfect Meal

Scorched Earth: A Political Love Story

Malaria Dreams: An African Adventure

*Night Train to Turkistan: Modern Adventures
Along China's Ancient Silk Road*

IT WAS ALL A LIE

IT WAS ALL A LIE

HOW THE REPUBLICAN PARTY
BECAME DONALD TRUMP

STUART STEVENS

ALFRED A. KNOPF NEW YORK 2020

Library of Congress Cataloging-in-Publication Data

Names: Stevens, Stuart, author.
Title: It was all a lie : how the Republican Party
became Donald Trump / Stuart Stevens.
Description: First edition. | New York : Alfred A. Knopf,
2020. | "This is a Borzoi book published by Alfred A.
Knopf." | Includes bibliographical references.
Identifiers: LCCN 2019048755 | ISBN 9780525658450
(hardcover) | ISBN 9780525658467 (ebook)
Subjects: LCSH: Trump, Donald, 1946– | Republican Party
(U.S. : 1854–)—History. | Conservatism—United States—History. |
Political culture—United States—History. | United States—Politics and
government—1945–1989. | United States—Politics and government—
1989– Classification: LCC JK2356 .S746 2020 | DDC 324.2734—dc23
LC record available at https://lccn.loc.gov/2019048755

Jacket art and design by Chip Kidd

Manufactured in the United States of America

Published August 4, 2020
Reprinted One Time
Third Printing, August 2020

*To the Deep State patriots who
are defending America*

Sometimes party loyalty asks too much.

—PRESIDENT JOHN F. KENNEDY

CONTENTS

IT WAS ALL A LIE

PROLOGUE
IT WAS ALL A LIE

I have no one to blame but myself. I believed. That's where it all started to go wrong. I was drawn to a party that espoused a core set of values: character counts, personal responsibility, strong on Russia, the national debt actually mattered, immigration made America great, a big-tent party invited all. Legislation would come and go, compromises would be necessary, but these principles were assumed to be shared and defined what it meant to be a Republican for the last fifty years.

What a fool I was. All of these immutable truths turned out to be mere marketing slogans. None of it meant anything. I was the guy working for Bernie Madoff who actually thought we were really smart and just crushing the market. What I missed was one simple reality: it was all a lie.

I come to this not out of bitterness but out of sadness. It's not that I failed. I was paid to win races for Republicans, and while I didn't win every race, I had the best win-loss record of anyone in my business. So yes, blame me. Blame me when you look around and see a dysfunctional political system and a Republican Party that has gone insane. To be sure, others share blame, but if there is any sane path forward for something resembling a conservative governing philosophy in America—and I'm not sure there is—it must start with honesty and accountability. I have this crazy idea that a return to personal responsibility begins with personal responsibility.

It is a strange, melancholy feeling to turn sixty-five and realize that what you have spent a good portion of your life working for and toward was not only meritless but also destructive. Among the many Republicans who find Donald Trump somewhere between distasteful and abhorrent, there are two distinct tendencies. One is to say that Trump isn't a real Republican. The other is to say he is just an "unconventional president" and focus on his policies.

Both are wrong.

As much as I'd love to go to bed at night reassuring myself that Donald Trump was some freak product of the system—a "black swan," as his ludicrously unqualified son-in-law says—I can't do it. I can't keep lying to myself to ward off the depressing reality that I had been lying to myself for decades. There is nothing strange or unexpected about Donald Trump. He is the logical conclusion of what the Republican Party became over the last fifty or so years, a natural product of the seeds of race, self-deception, and anger that became the essence of the Republican Party. Trump isn't an aberration of the Republican Party; he *is* the Republican Party in a purified form.

I saw the warning signs but ignored them and chose to believe what I wanted to believe: the party wasn't just a white grievance party; there was still a big tent; the other guys were worse. Mostly, though, I just didn't think about it. I loved to win and I won a lot. I loved the feeling that I had a big lever and could move if not the world, then a big enough hunk of it to make a difference.

Donald Trump didn't hijack the Republican Party and force it to bend to his will, abandoning so many avowed "bedrock" principles. How do I know this? I was there and, yes, I contributed. This is not an "I am better than them" plea. I'm not. But I was more than just a witness to this. I spent 2016 predicting that Donald Trump would not win because I refused to believe what Donald Trump proved about Republicans, about myself, could be true.

I was wrong.

Hold Donald Trump up to the mirror and that bulging, grotesque orange face *is* today's Republican Party. Working intensely in politics is joining a tribe, and if you do it for many years, a comfortable familiarity begins to define the experience. Do it professionally at a high level with success, and at a certain point you look around and you know where you belong in that tribe. Every two years you work in governor and Senate races, and every four years you probably end up toward the top of a presidential campaign. I've worked in five presidential races. Four out of five we won the nomination. Two out of five we won it all.

This is a book I never thought I'd write, that I didn't want to write. But it's the book I now must write. It's a truth to which I can bear witness. Many will argue that my view of the Republican Party is distorted by my loathing of Trump. The truth is that Trump brought it all into clarity and made the pretending impossible.

A word of caution on what this book is not. Those looking

for this to be a detailed indictment of sins and horrors committed by those I worked for and with will be disappointed. I am not writing to settle scores or name names. This is no bill of indictment to prepare for the political war crimes trials of the future. There is a collective blame shared by those of us who have created the modern Republican Party that has so egregiously failed the principles it claimed to represent. My *j'accuse* is against us all, not a few individuals who were the most egregious.

Yes, it was all a lie. But this is the truth.

1

RACE, THE ORIGINAL
REPUBLICAN SIN

You start out in 1954 by saying, "Nigger, nigger,
nigger." By 1968 you can't say "nigger"—that hurts
you. Backfires. So you say stuff like forced busing,
states' rights and all that stuff.

—Lee Atwater, 1981[1]

I played the race card in my very first race.

It was 1978 and my first client was running for Congress
in Mississippi. His name was Jon Hinson. He had been chief
of staff to a Mississippi congressman named Thad Cochran,
who was now running for the Senate. (Actually, back then they
called the head staffers "administrative assistants," or AAs,
but as government became more about positioning for that
next job and less about service, that sounded too much like
"secretaries," so the more elevated "chief of staff" became
common. What lobbying shop wants to pay $500,000 for a
former AA?) In high school I had been a page when Hinson
ran the congressional office, and I'd kept in touch when visit-
ing the office on trips to D.C.

Hinson was running against the son of Senator John
Stennis, a Mississippi icon of the Democratic Party. The son,

John Hampton Stennis, was a state representative, and it was assumed he would win easily. I was in film school then at UCLA, and Hinson called and asked if I could make television commercials for his campaign. I told him I didn't know how to make commercials, that I just made silly little films and wrote scripts I couldn't sell. "That doesn't matter," he said. "You have to do it. I can't afford to pay anyone who does this for real." In retrospect, this might not have been the most compelling pitch. But like anyone who has gone to film school, I was eager to get out and actually do something even vaguely related to film, so I said yes.

I'd been one of those kids who loved politics and campaigns and had walked precincts since the 1967 "William Winter for Governor" campaign in Mississippi. Winter ran against the last avowed segregationist to be elected governor, John Bell Williams, and it was a race full of death threats and drama. Winter lost, but I fell in love with politics and read Teddy White's *Making of the President, 1960* over and over.[2] It seemed a strange and intoxicating world, and when I left film school and started working in the Hinson campaign, I instantly felt at home. There was this sense of doing something that might actually *matter*. If I came up with the right ad, I might make a little history—or at least that's what I told myself. It was the tiniest bit of history—a Mississippi congressional seat—but it seemed infinitely more consequential than student films and debating what was the greatest opening camera move in cinema. The only problem was we were losing.

Stennis was a towering figure in Mississippi, and his name on the ballot was the obvious default choice for voters. Hinson was right when he said he couldn't afford to hire anyone, because no one thought he would win and for good reason. We raised some money, put up a few positive ads, and moved comfortably into second place, which is where we seemed stuck. The problem was that the congressional district, which included a lot of Jackson, Mississippi, and Vicksburg, was around 30 percent African American and, true to form, Hinson was getting less than 10 percent of that vote.

Thad Cochran was facing the same problem in his Senate race. No Republican had been elected statewide in Mississippi since Reconstruction, mostly because there really wasn't much of a functioning Republican Party in Mississippi. Cochran had won a congressional race against a very weak Democrat and then relied on incumbency to win easy races, but every other member of the Mississippi congressional delegation was Democratic. In his Senate race, Cochran had one great advantage: Charles Evers, the brother of the assassinated civil rights leader Medgar Evers, was running as an independent. Not surprisingly, he was drawing a significant portion of the African American vote. With the bulk of the black vote going to a third-party candidate, the race between the Republican and the Democrat largely came down to a fight for white voters. And that was a fight Cochran was winning. He was a young, likable attorney from Jackson and had a strong base in his former congressional district. Evers had no chance of winning, but he was enabling Cochran to move into first place.

What we needed in the Hinson campaign was a like dynamic of an independent African American drawing black votes from the Democrat. And we had one: Evan Doss Jr., a thirty-year-old African American, had qualified to run as an independent for the congressional seat. The problem was that he wasn't famous like Charles Evers, so few, including those in the black community, knew he was running. So I did the obvious thing: I made ads that showed the Republican, the Democrat, and independent, Evan Doss. I did it like a public service announcement: "In the Fourth Congressional District, three candidates are running." I put all three on the screen with their names. "Jon Hinson is the Republican nominee. John Hampton Stennis is the Democratic nominee. Evan Doss is running as an independent and would be the first African American candidate elected to Congress in Mississippi since Reconstruction."

That was it. I thought it was terribly clever, and it didn't bother me a bit on any "I'm playing the race card" kind of level. What could be wrong with informing voters of the choice they faced? And it worked beautifully. On Election Day, Hinson won with 51.6 percent of the vote followed by John Hampton Stennis with 26.4 percent and Evan Doss with 19 percent.[3] Every vote for Doss was a vote that would have gone to Stennis. In the end, Hinson might have won without the black independent, but it would have been very, very close.

In my first race I had stumbled onto a truth as basic and immutable as the fact that water freezes below thirty-two degrees Fahrenheit: race was the key in which much of American politics and certainly all of southern politics was played. It was really very simple: the Democratic candidate needed

90-plus percent of black votes to win. If a significant portion voted for a third party, the Republican would win.

It hadn't always been this way. Before 1964, Republican presidential candidates could expect to get between 30 and 40 percent of the African American vote. Dwight Eisenhower got 39 percent in 1956. Four years later, Richard Nixon campaigned with Jackie Robinson and won 32 percent of black voters. In 1964, Barry Goldwater opposed the Civil Rights Act, and his black support plummeted to 7 percent. Since 1964, no Republican presidential candidate has broken 17 percent with African American voters, and by 2016 only 3 percent considered themselves Republican.[4]

Politics is in many ways a perfect marketplace. Candidates and parties learn very quickly what works and what doesn't and focus time, energy, and money on the share of the marketplace that pollsters tell them is accessible to persuasion or motivation. Since 1964, Republicans have learned that they will have little success in appealing to black voters. It's not that most campaigns didn't make at least some effort, but it was always done with the knowledge that breaking 10 percent would be a significant achievement.

What happens if you spend decades focused on appealing to white voters and treating nonwhite voters with, at best, benign neglect? You get good at doing what it takes to appeal to white voters. That is the truth that led to what is famously called "the southern strategy." That is the path that leads you to becoming what the Republican Party now proudly embraces: a white grievance party.

All my adult life in politics, I've heard Republicans blame

our problems with black voters on "how" we communicated with the "minority community." The Republican Party has hired an entire cottage industry of black consultants to help candidates, campaigns, and elected officials crack the code of how to talk to African Americans, as if there were some linguistic issue blocking the party from returning to the party of Abraham Lincoln. It's all nonsense, and black voters get that it's nonsense.

The reason African Americans overwhelmingly reject Republicans isn't based on word choices or phrasing. It's based on policy. It isn't *how* Republicans are talking to black voters that results in 90 percent or more of those voters refusing to vote for Republicans. It's *what* the Republicans are doing, once elected. The fact that the Republican establishment is so invested in the myth that their problems are a matter of language is revealing and self-damning. At the root of it is a deep condescension that they—the de facto White Party of America—know what is best for black folks, and it's unfortunate these black folks don't seem to get it but, you know, they are different and we have to talk to them in a language they can understand.

The reality is just the opposite. Since 1964, black voters have heard the Republican Party with exquisite clarity; more important, they have seen what Republicans are doing once in office. It's summed up nicely in a chapter called "The GOP's Rise as 'the White Man's Party'" in *Dog Whistle Politics* by Ian Haney López: "Where in 1962 both parties were perceived as equally, if tepidly, supportive of civil rights, two years later 60 percent of the public identified Democrats as more likely to pursue fair treatment, versus only 7 percent who so identified the Republican Party."[5] Barry Goldwater ran on a carefully crafted platform of coded racism that contradicted his previous support of civil rights legislation. As Walter De Vries and Jack Bass wrote in the 1978 *Emerging Coalitions in American Politics,*

> The Republican decision to exploit the race issue and abandon the option of becoming a party of reform manifested itself in the 1961 speech in Atlanta by Barry Goldwater to a gathering of Southern Republicans. "We're not going to get the Negro vote as a bloc in 1964 and 1968, so we ought to go hunting where the ducks are," he declared. Goldwater then spelled it out, saying that school integration was "the responsibility of the states. I would not like to see my party assume it is the role of the federal government to enforce integration in the schools."[6]

The "ducks" were white voters, and in 1964, of the six states Goldwater carried, five were in the old Confederacy (the other being his home state of Arizona). African American support for Republicans fell off a cliff in 1964 and has never returned. As Hispanic and other nonwhite support plummets for Republicans, I hear many in the party assure themselves it is temporary and will "bounce back" as soon as the "right" leader emerges for the party. That's a hopeful fantasy, as the example of 1964 proves.

When Jon Hinson beat Senator Stennis's son in my first

congressional race, it received some attention in national political circles as an upset. Suddenly I found candidates interested in hiring me to make television commercials for their campaigns. It was how I stumbled into becoming a political consultant. I found I could work in campaigns for a short time and have the off-season to try to write books and articles. At the time no one would pay me much to write, so it was an easy way to make a living doing what was in effect seasonal work, sort of like migrant labor work but indoors and a lot easier.

A few years later I was working in the first congressional campaign for a young Florida banker named Connie Mack. He was running in a newly created district around Fort Myers, Florida, that was created to be a safe Republican seat. His toughest campaign was in the Republican primary, and after that it seemed fairly certain he would win the general election. (He went on to win with 65 percent of the vote.) It was a predominantly white district, but for some reason the Republican National Committee sent down an African American consultant to coach the campaign and candidate on how to maximize appeal to black voters. It was hyped as a "highly important" meeting with a great drumroll from Washington.

I was still naive enough to think there might be some secret language we could learn that would allow us to move the hearts of at least a substantial number of black voters. We had a simple storefront campaign headquarters. It reminded me of the scenes from Teddy White's *Making of the President,* and every time I walked into it, I felt like a character of White's, playing out in my head the drama of coming behind in the West Virginia primary when Kennedy beat Humphrey.

It made the endeavor seem far grander than a routine election of a nice-guy banker who had run mostly because he was bored and had a name that still meant something to the older snowbirds in the district. (Connie Mack's grandfather and namesake managed the Philadelphia Athletics for their first fifty seasons.) Our pollster, Arthur Finkelstein, an intense mad genius who had specialized in electing hard-right candidates like Jesse Helms, muttered to Connie in one poll briefing, "Every time an ambulance goes by, you lose a voter."

For this critical meeting with the African American consultant, we were summoned to a small conference room at a local hotel. It was an all-day meeting and catered. I had never been to a catered meeting before. Our small staff gathered with Connie and his wife and the RNC consultant. He was dressed impeccably in an elegant suit with a blue shirt that had a white collar. He was wearing Gucci loafers, which I wouldn't have known except later one of the young staffers, who was gay, noted with grudging admiration that they were nice shoes. (Just about every Republican campaign I've worked on had a sizable gay contingent of staffers. The more conservative the candidate, the greater seemed the percentage of gay staffers. The correlation between the conservatism of a Republican candidate and the number of gay staffers seems so reliable that in a later campaign when there was discussion among the staff of the candidate's sexual orientation, I could declare with some certainty, "I don't think our guy is conservative enough to be gay." The point was accepted, and I later heard a young press operative trying to explain this to a baffled reporter who, thank God, did not quote him.)

In 1982, there was near 10 percent unemployment nationally, and jobs were the number one issue in just about every race, including the Thirteenth District of Florida. The RNC consultant, who had a deep, resonating voice, began by saying that black voters were just like white voters in that what they cared about were good jobs and a stronger economy. Since then, in my decades working in Republican politics, I have heard variations on this theme countless times, referring to black voters, Hispanic voters, Asian voters—any nonwhite voters: they care about the same issues as white voters. This is one of those insidious half-truths that conceal a deeper, more important truth. Yes, pretty much all voters do care about jobs. But to say a white college-educated male or female cared about jobs in the same way as an African American is delusional. It was akin to saying that everyone would like not to get shot and that this truth means the same to a white suburban high school student in Des Moines as it does to a black teenager in Chicago's K-Town. It was a truth asserted with such disregard for specifics that it became a building block of a larger falsehood. Feed generations of Republicans these easily digestible bromides, and it isn't hard to understand the failure of Republicans to grasp the meaning of Black Lives Matter. The cry "Don't all lives matter?" is just another variation on the assumption that jobs mean the same to all voters.

The one African American in the room stood before us and declared, "The issue in this race isn't black and white but green." At the time this phrase struck me as somewhat ingenious with a hint of the profound. Over the next thirty-some-odd years, I would hear this line over and over, even though Republicans kept losing black voters. But then I just nodded, as did everyone in the room, and smiled appreciatively at being graced with this wisdom. "It's good you are talking about jobs," the consultant said, directing it to Connie Mack. "But unless you change the way you talk about jobs, black folk just won't hear your message."

We hung on every word. I knew from our polling that the district's black voters favored the Democratic candidate on the jobs issue overwhelmingly, so there was no arguing that we were failing to reach these voters. The consultant from Washington was right.

"Here is how you get black voters to support you on jobs." He then turned to the whiteboard, where he had written "Good Jobs." With great deliberateness, he crossed out "Good" and wrote "Meaningful." "That's the key," he said. "Black voters don't believe you if you just talk about 'good' jobs. You need to talk about 'meaningful' jobs."

I'm embarrassed to say I furiously took notes. For the rest of the campaign, we tried to talk about "meaningful" jobs. Of course it meant nothing. Connie won the election and was crushed with black voters. Two years later, the man known as "the great communicator," Ronald Reagan, won forty-nine states. But, like Connie, he was crushed with black voters, who went for Walter Mondale at over 90 percent.

Today, in the age of Donald Trump, the most openly racist president since Andrew Johnson or his hero Andrew Jackson (to the extent a know-nothing narcissist is capable of having a hero), many Republicans who find Trump repulsive or at least consider him abrasive and uncouth hark back to Reagan as the standard compared with whom Trump is woefully inadequate.

This is true in areas like foreign policy, where the Republican Party has gone from "Mr. Gorbachev, tear down this wall!" to a Republican president who responds to Vladimir Putin like a stray dog, eager to follow him home. But in the area of race, there is a direct line from the more genteel prejudice of Ronald Reagan to the white nationalism of Donald Trump. In the glow of nostalgia around a smiling Reagan faded into the California sunset, Republicans have forgotten, have discounted, or, perhaps for some, still secretly admire that Ronald Reagan wielded race as a magnet to attract disaffected white Democrats. When Reagan attacked "welfare queens," white voters heard it and understood the unspoken accusation just as they did when George Wallace did the same. In the 1976 campaign, Reagan introduced his famous welfare fraud, a black woman in Chicago: "She used 80 names, 30 addresses, 15 telephone numbers to collect food stamps, Social Security, veterans' benefits for four nonexistent deceased veteran husbands, as well as welfare. Her tax-free cash income alone has been running $150,000 a year."[7] Reagan's "welfare queen" was likely an exaggerated description of a woman exposed in 1974 articles in both the *Chicago Tribune* and *Jet* magazine. As much as many of us—yes, I include myself in this group—would like to, even need to, separate Reagan from Trump, the welfare-queen theme weaponized race and deceit in exactly the same ways employed by Donald Trump. There is a small kernel of truth in it—the woman used four, not eighty names, and the total fraud was $8,000—but when four becomes eighty and $8,000 total becomes $150,000 a year, Reagan is just lying. The majority of all welfare goes to white Americans and always has, but the specificity of a woman in Chicago makes the racial appeal clear.

In the 2012 Romney campaign, I made several ads about welfare reform. The impetus was a waiver that the Obama administration gave in the summer of 2012 to states that allowed them to reduce or eliminate work requirements. The result was a firestorm of criticism. Our argument was that Barack Obama had never been enthusiastic about the Clinton welfare reforms in the 1990s—he opposed them when they were first introduced, and in the 2008 campaign refused to say if he would have signed them into law if he was president—and that this was a deliberately vague back door to allowing states to reduce work for welfare requirements. It was put best by Douglas Besharov, a public policy professor at the University of Maryland, who is credited with helping persuade Hillary Clinton to support the 1996 law. He was quoted in an article by the *Chicago Tribune* columnist Steve Chapman:

"If the Obama administration believes in work requirements, why write something so broad?" Besharov asked me. "If I believed in the work requirements, I wouldn't put in language encouraging states to lift them all."[8]

In the Romney campaign, we saw this as a specific example of different governing philosophies. As Molly Ball wrote in

The Atlantic, "It's not much of a stretch to conclude that the waivers the administration is soliciting, if they come to pass, would result in more people getting welfare benefits. The question is whether that's a good thing, and where you stand on that depends on your politics."[9]

That was the fight we wanted to be in, a differing governing philosophy about the role of government. In Massachusetts, where I worked in governor races for William Weld, his position on welfare reform had been central to his campaigns, and the debate with his opponents had not been supercharged with allegations of racism. But that was a governor's race between two white opponents. I should have realized that any discussion of welfare in a national campaign, particularly in a presidential race between a white candidate and an African American president, was nearly impossible without its being dominated by racial overtones. The reality is that there is an ugly history of code words and dog whistles in the party, and it's something Republicans must admit and address. When Ronald Reagan campaigned in Mississippi at the Neshoba County Fair in 1980, I was quick to defend him against charges of race-baiting. Yes, Neshoba County had the horrible legacy of three civil rights workers murdered and buried in a dam in 1964, but I had grown up going to the Neshoba County Fair hearing politicians speak. It was a ritual of passage, like town halls and house parties in New Hampshire. That a future president would speak there was to be celebrated, not criticized.

But I was wrong. Reagan did not give an explicitly racist speech, but the totality of the place and what he said—and didn't say—was a direct racist appeal to white Mississippi voters. In a county where black and white Americans had been assassinated trying to earn the right for other Americans to vote, a presidential candidate failed to mention the debt owed to these heroes. Clichéd as it may be, context really is everything. It is one thing to speak of "states' rights" in a debate on the meaning of the Tenth Amendment to the Constitution. It's another to speak of it as Reagan did at Neshoba when he declared, "I believe in state's rights."[10] Jimmy Carter had carried the state in 1976 by less than 2 percent. Knowing that his appeal to black voters had a very low ceiling, Reagan needed to attract white voters who had gone for Carter in 1976. He did, winning Mississippi by a handful of votes. A map of the precincts carried by Carter versus Reagan says it all: Carter carried black Mississippi; Reagan carried white.

Thirty-seven years later, Donald Trump would stand in another state, Alabama, where civil rights was a life-and-death struggle, and attack NFL players protesting police brutality by taking a knee during the national anthem. "That's a total disrespect of our heritage. That's a total disrespect of everything that we stand for. Wouldn't you love to see one of these NFL owners, when somebody disrespects our flag, you'd say, 'Get that son of a bitch off the field right now. Out! He's fired.' "[11] In a state where more than three hundred African Americans were lynched, many for the simple crime of trying to vote or helping others vote, referencing "our heritage" and calling black protesters sons of bitches in front of an overwhelmingly white audience was the perfect kind of racial pitch. It was heard clearly and undeniably as racist.

In many ways, the 2017 Alabama special election to replace Senator Jeff Sessions was a barometer of current racial politics in our two-party system. It was a gut check of what it would take to separate today's Republicans from their party's choice. Even given the choice of supporting an alleged child molester with a troubled, to say the least, history on race or a moderate Democrat, 68 percent of white Alabama voters stuck with the alleged child molester. Only African American voters, particularly African American women, saved Alabama from itself.[12]

Since Trump's nomination, I've had many long, painful talks with Republicans I've known and worked with for decades. In my tribe there is a general sense of dismay but an understandable reluctance among most to blame the modern evolution of the party as a white party. I often hear, "Look at Bill Clinton: He ran on reforming welfare and the death penalty. Why isn't that racist? If welfare is code and blacks are much more likely to be on death row, isn't Clinton playing the race card?"

The answer is yes, of course Clinton played racial politics. After Michael Dukakis's defeat, in part due to the Willie Horton attacks, Clinton had made a deliberate choice to redefine his party. The Clinton slogan "A different kind of Democrat" was a direct message to the white voters who had abandoned the party. Clinton doubled down on southern appeal with Al Gore, and the two took their Southern Good Ole Boy act across the old Confederacy. Clinton won Louisiana, Tennessee, Kentucky, and Arkansas, all states George H. W. Bush had won easily in 1988.

So what's the difference between Clinton's making a racial appeal in 1992 and Bush's doing the same in 1988 with the Willie Horton attack? The answer is simple and one African American voters seem to understand with great clarity: The modern Democratic Party has fought for civil rights and believes government has a moral role in helping to create racial equality in America. The modern Republican Party has fought civil rights and is very hesitant to assert government has a role in equality of any sort, including racial.

What do I mean by the "modern" Republican Party? It's the party we have today that is the culmination of a long victory march of the conservative and right-wing elements that were once balanced in part by moderates. The 1966 postelection cover of *Time* magazine was titled "Republican Resurgence" and had on the cover Governor Ronald Reagan of California, Governor George Romney of Michigan, Senator Chuck Percy of Illinois, Senator Mark Hatfield of Oregon, Senator Ed Brooke of Massachusetts, and Governor Nelson Rockefeller of New York. This group was heralded as saving the Republican Party after the disaster of Goldwater in 1964. With the exception of Reagan, all defined themselves as moderate problem solvers eager to work with Democrats. None, absent Reagan, considered themselves conservative ideologues.

That Republican Party as a national institution is dead. There are similar Republican governors today—Larry Hogan of Maryland, Phil Scott of Vermont, Charlie Baker of Massachusetts—but the national GOP, at best, treats them with benign neglect. This is, of course, insane. These governors are all wildly popular. For a political party that espouses to admire business so much and wants to run government like a business, ignoring those who are selling like crazy in the toughest markets is self-defeating but very telling. The RNC endorsed Roy Moore but ignores moderate governors. What else do you need to know?

The path followed by the two major parties today was laid by each in the 1960s. In 1964, George Wallace ran against Lyndon Johnson after the notoriety he had gained for "standing in the schoolhouse door" when the University of Alabama was integrated.[13] (We now know this was carefully orchestrated with Attorney General Bobby Kennedy.) He entered three primaries—Wisconsin, Indiana, and Maryland—and won about a third of the vote. The same year, Goldwater was the conservative candidate in the Republican primary, while moderates desperately tried to settle on one candidate to oppose him. Governors William Scranton of Pennsylvania, Nelson Rockefeller of New York, and George Romney of Michigan split the moderate votes, and Goldwater won easily. At the Democratic National Convention, there was a fight over which delegates to seat from Mississippi: the all-white (and segregationist) Democratic Party regulars or the integrated Mississippi Freedom Democratic Party. A compromise was struck that largely hid the deep division between the two. Goldwater carried only states from the Confederacy, plus Arizona.

But what if George Wallace had won the Democratic primary? What if the Democratic establishment had then accepted Wallace? It's safe to say the Democratic Party would not resemble its current form. The rejection of Wallace was as much a statement for the Democratic Party as the acceptance by Trump of the Republican Party.

It isn't hard to argue that the Democratic Party has often disappointed the trust placed in it by African American voters. The Hillary Clinton campaign of 2016 was in many ways running against the Bill Clinton campaign of 1992. He campaigned on the death penalty and pushed federal funding to help pay for 100,000 more cops, largely in urban areas, with the result that the incarceration rate of African Americans increased dramatically. Hillary Clinton made "mass incarceration" an issue, and the mothers of slain black youths spoke at the 2016 Democratic National Convention.

During an NBC interview in 1979, Bayard Rustin, one of the organizers of Martin Luther King's March on Washington and one of the more fascinating figures in the civil rights movement, was blunt about frustrations with the civil rights bill and its aftermath:

> People have to understand that although the civil rights bill was good and something for which I worked arduously, there was nothing in it that had any effect whatsoever on the three major problems Negroes face in the North: housing, jobs, and integrated schools. . . . [T]he civil-rights bill, because of this failure, has caused an even deeper frustration in the North.[14]

But the inadequacy of legislation supported by Democrats is far different from a calculated effort to appeal to white voters by manipulating the race issue. One is a failure of policy. The other is a moral failure. In an October 5, 1971, White House memorandum from "Research" to the White House chief of staff, H. R. Haldeman, headed "Dividing the Democrats," the authors went through various elaborate ways the Nixon White House and campaign could manipulate racism to help Nixon's reelection campaign. It was written by

Pat Buchanan and Kevin Phillips, who both went on to play pivotal roles in the development of the party, and it was based on the assumption there was little Nixon could do to attract black voters, so the focus should be on utilizing black voters' support of Democrats to alienate white voters. The memo is a playbook for how best to play the race card, and Republican candidates have used similar tactics for decades. As Buchanan and Phillips recommended to Nixon,

> Fourth Party Candidates: Top-level consideration should be given to ways and means to promote, assist and fund a Fourth Party candidacy of the Left Democrats and/or the Black Democrats. There is nothing that can so advance the President's chances for re-election—not a trip to China, not four-and-a-half percent unemployment—as a realistic black Presidential candidate.

The memo voiced frustration at not being able to communicate a positive message to black voters and a sense of resentment that Nixon's efforts at outreach to black voters had gone unappreciated. It concluded that nothing positive would have much effect, so the logical and best course was to minimize the impact of black voters in various ways. This was the Nixon strategy in 1972. It was the Trump strategy in 2016. It was so obvious that even the Russians adopted it, attempting to instigate tensions among black voters to help Trump win. The memo continues,

> Note: Since taking office, the President has increased by 500 percent—from $400 million to $2 billion—the

food stamp and food assistance funding and he still gets it in the neck for "starving the poor." Methinks there would have been more gratitude and greater awards if these funds had been directed to the President's potential friends in the working class, and their interests.

Black Complaints: As we did with Muskie we should continue to champion the cause of the Blacks within the Democratic Party; elevate their complaint of "being taken for granted."[15]

One of the common traits of the Republican Party, which the media seems to often accept and imitate, is the discussion of "the working class" as if it were the white working class. It reduces African Americans and other nonwhites to invisible and nonexistent and is a perfect example of the casual racism of so much of conservative politics. Here the Nixon White House articulates the pattern in classic style:

If the President would become the visible and outspoken champion of the Forgotten American, the working people of this country—and assert that the welfare types have been taken care of for years; it would force a division within the Democratic Party, would align the media against us—but methinks it both divides them and assists us.[16]

The most "forgotten Americans" are the nonwhite Americans. But by calling out to the white Americans who feel slighted or frustrated by their lot in life, Nixon was mining the same resentment vein that Trump—and George Wallace—

exploited. It has been a common Republican ploy to paint Democrats as the victim shoppers, the easily offended, the "snowflakes" of society, while the Republicans have been masters of proclaiming the virtues of personal responsibility, at least until Trump, whose eternal state is claiming he is victimized.

When Trump first emerged and positioned himself as a warrior for the oppressed white people of America, I argued, along with others, that this was a stark aberration of the position long held by Republicans of belief in "personal responsibility." I clung to the notion that Republicans believed Ronald Reagan when he declared, "We must reject the idea that every time a law's broken, society is guilty rather than the lawbreaker. It is time to restore the American precept that each individual is accountable for his actions."[17] I was half-right. Republicans did still believe in what Reagan said. But to most of them, it meant society should hold responsible those who they believe are most likely to break the law, that is, blacks or other nonwhites like the Mexican "rapists" Trump railed against when launching his campaign.[18] The same did not apply to whites. So many Republicans embraced Trump's view that they were victims, as was he, because they had actually believed this all along. Theirs was a white birthright, and the rise of nonwhites was an unjust usurping of their rights.

The similarities of George Wallace and Donald Trump are striking, from attacking the news media to railing against elites, all played in the key of racism. This isn't an aberration or a sudden wrong turn by the Republican Party. The Nixon White House studied Wallace and deliberately tried to mobilize his race-based support without alienating voters who were uncomfortable with Wallace's style. The Buchanan-Phillips memo outlines the approach:

Regional Fissures: South versus North. Here the dividing line is essentially that of the race issue; but it goes further into the "liberalism" of the national Democratic Party leaders, and major candidates, which does not sit well with the essential "suburban conservatism" and even "Wallaceism" of Democrats in the South. To force a choice here, we need more than just rhetoric and mailings. Actions taken by the President and Administration are decisive here.[19]

To their "credit," the Nixon White House realized that the core of playing the race card was about substantive legislative and judicial choices, not merely language:

The Supreme Court nomination of a Southern Strict Constructionist will force Democratic Northern liberals, and major candidates, to anger either the South with a voice vote, or the blacks and the labor movement and the Northern liberals. A highly qualified Southern Conservative nominee to the Supreme Court is de facto a divisive issue in the Democratic Party.

Elevation of the issue of compulsory school integration and neighborhood integration, via such as "bussing" and the Ribicoff Plan. Clearly, this puts Northern liberals like Muskie on an untenable hook. And with the Detroit horror show shaping up, this is going to be even more a national "voting" issue. Mr. Wallace has recognized this.

The serious problem here was that while Muskie might have been in favor of compulsory integration by his votes, the administration was the one seen as in power while various odious rulings and policies were being enforced. The memo continued,

> Many of my sources tell me that it is the President—since he is visible in office, and has made strong statements— who is today being hurt worst by the busing fiasco. That is not as it should be, as I understand that the President's political and moral position is that it is wrong and contra-productive to forcibly integrate the races.
>
> However, if we are able to draw a line between us and the Democratic liberals, which leaves the Democratic conservatives on our side of the line—then action will be required, in my judgment, on the President's part.
>
> Frankly, this requires the kind of historic decision, bringing a constitutional end to the national pressure to integrate races in housing and schooling—which requires a decision on the part of the President. This would really tear up the pea patch; and our current policy is one of accommodation with the courts and confrontation.
>
> In conclusion, this is a potential throw of the dice

that could bring the media on our heads and cut the Democratic Party and country in half. My view is that we would have the far larger half, but that is not my decision.[20]

So the Nixon White House laid out the path to electoral success by maximizing white grievance and suppressing the African American vote through a combination of manipulation, lies, and legal challenges. It was this road that the Republican Party took to the Trump White House. There is nothing new about Donald Trump. He hasn't invented a new politics or executed a brilliant and novel strategy. Barry Goldwater, George Wallace, Richard Nixon, and even Ronald Reagan played the same race-based politics of resentment. It is precisely Trump's predictability and, alas, inevitability that is so depressing.

◆

Race has defined the modern Republican Party. After Goldwater carried only southern states and received a record low of 7 percent of the black vote, the party faced a basic choice: do what was necessary to appeal to more nonwhite voters, or build a party to win with white voters. It chose the latter, and when most successfully executed, a race-based strategy was the foundation of many of the Republican Party's biggest victories, from Nixon to Trump. And fittingly, absent serious change, race will define the demise of the Republican Party to a regional, Sunbelt-based party.

That's not a controversial opinion. It's just math. In 1980, Ronald Reagan won a sweeping landslide of forty-four states with 55 percent of the white vote. In 2012, Mitt Romney lost with 59 percent of the white vote. Four years later, Donald Trump was able to win the Electoral College with the same percentage of the white vote as Romney, but for the first time in twenty years African American turnout actually decreased; third-party voting also increased over 2012. So Trump wins the White House with 46.1 percent of the popular vote, and Romney loses with 47.2 percent.

After Romney's loss, the Republican Party appeared to realize it must change in order to survive as a national governing party. The Republican National Committee chairman, Reince Priebus, commissioned a so-called autopsy report to analyze why the party was struggling in presidential races:

> Republicans have lost the popular vote in five of the last six presidential elections. States in which our presidential candidates used to win, such as New Mexico, Colorado, Nevada, Iowa, Ohio, New Hampshire, Virginia, and Florida, are increasingly voting Democratic. We are losing in too many places.

Their assessment of the problem was not profound, but the problem was not profound; it was obvious:

> Public perception of the Party is at record lows. Young voters are increasingly rolling their eyes at what the Party represents, and many minorities wrongly think

that Republicans do not like them or want them in the country. When someone rolls their eyes at us, they are not likely to open their ears to us. At the federal level, much of what Republicans are doing is not working beyond the core constituencies that make up the Party.

The "autopsy" accurately described the political cliff the party was running toward, acknowledging that a party with little appeal to nonwhite voters was a party in great danger:

The nation's demographic changes add to the urgency of recognizing how precarious our position has become. America is changing demographically, and unless Republicans are able to grow our appeal the way GOP governors have done, the changes tilt the playing field even more in the Democratic direction. In 1980, exit polls tell us that the electorate was 88 percent white. In 2012, it was 72 percent white. Hispanics made up 7 percent of the electorate in 2000, 8 percent in 2004, 9 percent in 2008 and 10 percent in 2012. According to the Pew Hispanic Center, in 2050, whites will be 47 percent of the country while Hispanics will grow to 29 percent and Asians to 9 percent. If we want ethnic minority voters to support Republicans, we have to engage them and show our sincerity.[21]

This analysis is correct, of course, and credit should be given to a genuine effort to examine the problems of the party and be self-critical. But nowhere in the autopsy was there an acknowledgment or even consideration that the reason Republicans were failing with nonwhite voters was policy based, not just a question of demonstrating sincerity or failure to engage minorities. Nor is there any indication of the moral imperative of a political party that aspires to lead a country to be more inclusive and better reflect the country it seeks to represent. Perhaps that's too much to ask of a report commissioned by a political party to determine the political failures of that party. But I think it is telling that the Republican focus on the need to broaden the party has been driven by an instinct for survival and no real sense of a larger purpose.

This no doubt explains in part the alacrity with which the party abandoned every principle laid out in the autopsy once Donald Trump emerged as a dominant figure in the primary. How do you go from dedicating a political party to expansion and inclusiveness and two years later rally around a man who calls Mexicans "rapists" and called for a religious test to enter the United States? It's easy if you view an avowed commitment to inclusion as merely a political necessity and nothing more. For decades, conservatives attacked liberals for living by "situational ethics," but the ease with which Republican leaders abandoned any pretense of being more than a whites-only party is the ultimate situational ethic. It wasn't the morality of inclusion driving the call to expand the party; it was the political necessity. With Trump's victory in 2016, the party seemed to breathe a sigh of relief that no longer did it need to pretend that it must reach out more to nonwhite voters.

In the American political system, the major political parties should serve a "circuit breaker" function to deny the exploitation of the darkest side of our politics. The Republican Party did it in 2012 when it served notice that it would not support Todd Akin, the Missouri Republican nominee for U.S. Senate, after he answered a question on his opposition to abortion even in cases of rape:

> First of all, from what I understand from doctors, that's really rare. If it's a legitimate rape, the female body has ways to try to shut that whole thing down. But let's assume that maybe that didn't work or something. I think there should be some punishment, but the punishment ought to be on the rapist and not attacking the child.[22]

With a Senate nominee voicing an opinion on "legitimate rape," the chairman of the Republican National Committee, Reince Priebus, called on Akin to withdraw from the race and blocked any official party support for him. But four years later, Donald Trump called for a ban on Muslims' entering the United States, a clearly unconstitutional edict violating the Constitution's Article VI clause against a religious test, and the Republican Party leadership did nothing. When asked to respond, Priebus told the *Washington Examiner,* "I don't agree. We need to aggressively take on radical Islamic terrorism but not at the expense of our American values."[23] But there was no call for Trump to reverse his position or attempt to mobilize support against unconstitutional religious bigotry.

Why? The Republican Party was—and still is—afraid of Donald Trump. Early in the primary season, his threats to run as an independent neutralized any hint of courage the Republican Party establishment might have been able to muster. Then, as the primaries unfolded and the Republican version of George Wallace gained support, the leaders in the party quietly abandoned their principles and fell in line behind Donald Trump. Even when Mitt Romney stepped forward and called out Trump for what he clearly was—"a phony, a fraud. His promises are as worthless as a degree from Trump University"[24]—no other Republicans of note rallied behind him to speak publicly what most were saying privately.

How do you abandon deeply held beliefs about character, personal responsibility, foreign policy, and the national debt in a matter of months? You don't. The obvious answer is those beliefs weren't deeply held. In the end, the Republican Party rallied behind Donald Trump because if that was the deal needed to regain power, what was the problem? Because it had always been about power.

The rest? The principles? The values? It was all a lie.

2

FAMILY VALUES

I almost laugh out loud when I hear Democrats saying things like "Jesus said suffer the little children to come unto me" and try to use that as the reason we should open up our borders.

—Jerry Falwell Jr.[1]

Evangelicals still believe in the commandment, "Thou shalt not have sex with a porn star." . . . However, whether the president violated that commandment or not is totally irrelevant for our support of him.

—Robert Jeffress[2]

There's something I should have told you," the congressman said in a flat voice. This was before cell phones, and he had somehow tracked me down by phone in a Midas Muffler shop. Later, as my career developed, I would learn these are the worst seven words a client ever utters. Whatever follows will be somewhere between the merely disastrous and the fatal.

The congressman proceeded to tell me that when he was working as a staffer for the previous congressman, whom he replaced, he had been arrested at the Iwo Jima Memorial in

Arlington, Virginia, for indecent behavior. That was how he phrased it, "indecent behavior." I'm embarrassed to admit that I had no idea what he was trying to say. This couldn't have made it easier on him. "What do you mean?" I asked. There was a pause, and then, to his credit, he laughed. "You're not joking just to make this harder, are you?" And then, for some reason, it connected. I digested it the way I was beginning to learn to do as a consultant, without any thought of the incident itself or any sympathy for the client but in a clinical analysis of the various options moving forward.

Then he said what I have learned are the worst three words: "But there's more." And there was. The newly elected congressman went on to describe how he had left his job as chief of staff one afternoon and walked over to a gay porno theater, Cinema Follies, in the then-seedy part of Southeast Washington. It was upstairs over a storefront. During the film, a worker was cleaning the carpet on the stairs while smoking and accidentally ignited the cleaning fluid, engulfing the stairs in flames. Of the ten men inside the theater, only one survived—my client.

He was calling to tell me this because he believed that a possible future opponent had learned of both incidents and it might come out in the press. I vividly remember getting this call. Waiting for the muffler of my ancient Volvo to be repaired, I felt exhilarated, like a field goal kicker called on the field to win the game. I hope I expressed some sympathy for his near-death experience, but I'm sure that's not what I was thinking about. This was a problem, and it needed to be solved.

The solution was for the congressman to come forward and preempt any revelations by telling all to the press. It worked. Even in Mississippi, we were able to get him reelected. Then, a few months into his second term, he was arrested in a men's bathroom on the sixth floor of the Longworth Building, a floor that then was mainly storage areas. The congressional police force had heard it was a meeting place for gays and had staked it out, assuming, I would imagine, they would catch only staffers. Instead, they caught a newly reelected Congressman from Mississippi, Jon Hinson. Hinson resigned from Congress shortly after his arrest.

So I launched my career in the party that prided itself on being the "family values" party. When pundits marvel that the Republican Party could accept a man like Donald Trump, who has five kids from three wives and talks in public about having sex with his daughter, they're missing the point. Trump doesn't signal a lowering of standards of morality by Republican voters. Instead, he gives them a chance to prove how little they have always cared about those issues. Trump just removes the necessity of pretending. "Family values" was never a set of morals or values that the Republican Party really desired to live by; instead, "family values" was useful in attacking and defining Democrats. It was just another weapon to help portray those on the other side as being out of the mythical American mainstream. It was an "otherness" tool, as in those who didn't loudly proclaim their strict adherence to its code were "other" than normal. Like not being white is "other." Like not being Christian is "other." Like not being heterosexual is "other." The entire modern Republican definition of the conservative movement is about efforts to define itself as "normal" and everything else as "not normal."

The Republican use of "family values" was the weaponization of two key elements of its power structure: racial prejudice and a politically conservative Christianity, from Catholics to evangelicals. Seth Dowland summed it up perfectly in *Family Values and the Rise of the Christian Right:*

> In the early 1970s, white conservatives surveyed the American landscape and saw economic crises, spiraling crime, urban riots, and endless wars—both hot and cold. They determined that the nation had gone off the track. In particular, conservatives sensed that liberals had undermined traditional values. This climate was ripe for a politics that celebrated a nostalgic ideal of the home.[3]

For Republicans, that "home" invariably meant a gauzy view of an idealized America somewhere in the 1950s that never existed. Those roles continue to drive the structure of Republican politics and remain the key building blocks of the party's DNA. When Brett Kavanaugh testified in response to sexual assault allegations by Dr. Christine Blasey Ford, he painted a portrait of family life that was reassuringly out of the 1950s:

> During the weekdays in the summer of 1982, as you can see, I was out of town for two weeks of the summer for a trip to the beach with friends and at the legendary Five-Star Basketball Camp in Honesdale, Pennsylvania.

When I was in town, I spent much of my time working, working out, lifting weights, playing basketball, or hanging out and having some beers with friends as we talked about life, and football, and school and girls.

Some have noticed that I didn't have church on Sundays on my calendars. I also didn't list brushing my teeth. And for me, going to church on Sundays was like brushing my teeth, automatic. It still is.

The described world is one in which everyone knows their roles: a hermetically sealed world that could exist in any white American suburb. Though this world was perched on the edge of a predominantly African American city that had been torn apart by racial riots fifteen years earlier, it might as well have been Sioux City, Iowa, or Plano, Texas. Kavanaugh's audience for this homily was the Trump base that would assume if he lived such a life, he could not have assaulted a woman. He described a movie that white conservative voters could easily play in their heads, casting himself as the good boy whose idea of raising hell was drinking beer. It was a world without sex, as Kavanaugh describes it:

As to sex, this is not a topic I ever imagined would come up at a judicial confirmation hearing, but I want to give you a full picture of who I was. I never had sexual intercourse, or anything close to it, during high school, or for many years after that. In some crowds, I was probably a little outwardly shy about my inexperience; tried to hide that. At the same time, I was also inwardly proud of it.

For me and the girls who I was friends with, that lack of major rampant sexual activity in high school was a matter of faith and respect and caution.[4]

The family values that the Republican Party not only embraced as a personal ethos but wielded as a club against political opponents was built on the fantasy that sex did not exist. Liberals had sex, too much of it. Abortion would not be needed if men and women just quit having sex. Or any more sex than necessary to have children. The Equal Rights Amendment would not be needed if women would only accept their roles as defined by their sex, which was a far different thing from their sexuality. As Robert O. Self wrote in *All in the Family: The Realignment of American Democracy Since the 1960s,*

Behind the competing visions of American life were two ideas with far-reaching political consequences: citizens have *a* sex and they *have* sex. Prior to the second half of the twentieth century, the United States, like most societies in the West, rarely recognized the first proposition. Citizens were not imbued with the gender differences assigned by biology. The universal subject of modern democracies was assumed to be a white heterosexual male. Americans did recognize the second proposition, but its implications were hidden behind the all-important distinction between public and private so long employed to divide political from domestic life in classic political thinking. Even as the state regulated everything from women's reproduction to sexual behavior and marriage, sex and sexuality were imagined as private. They were thought to have no meaningful relationship to democratic citizenship.[5]

The Christian right would like the world to believe it was the political arm of Jesus Christ, come to life to save a sinful America. In practice it operates more like a Christian-related super PAC for a white America. The professional politicization of Christianity as a right-wing force was always more about the acquisition of power than a commitment to Christianity. It was where the commercialization of Christianity meets the politicization of Christianity. The long list of high-profile evangelical figures who scammed the public and lived their lives exactly opposite of what they preached reveals the essential truth of the Moral Majority and the like efforts it spawned. In *The Immoral Majority,* Ben Howe, an evangelical who grew up in the movement, describes the long list of disgraced preachers as "figures who were cartoonish, dramatic, deceitful, wealthy, white, smarmy, judgmental, callous, and, above all, hypocritical. Charlatans."[6] This is about as perfect a description of Donald Trump as one can find.

To understand how white evangelicals could embrace Donald Trump, consider him the ultimate white megachurch preacher. The congregation has been conditioned to accept leaders who are lying, philandering frauds who live extravagant lifestyles far above their own means. But even the larger-than-life flaws and sins of these men—and they are all men—serve to convince the flock that they are unworthy to judge such men. Their followers proudly claim they favor "authenticity" as a virtue but are drawn to the most elaborately artificial of men who cosmetically, chemically, and surgically alter their physical presence as if to affirm they were of a different, more godlike persona. Compare photographs of Jimmy Swaggart and Donald Trump, and they look like brothers from some strange union of Mardi Gras floats: huge heads, strange colors, balloon bodies, mouths disconnected from brains. The very strangeness of the figures makes them harder to judge by the standards of normal human behavior. Their entire artifice is to appear abnormal and thus escape judgment. These men are "different" and should be judged differently.

During the 2016 Republican primary, vast sums were spent by candidates other than Trump attacking one another rather than Trump. In retrospect, this seems quite insane, but at the time the theory made sense: Surely the Republican Party would not nominate a man who was in the casino business, had five children by three wives, and was a maxed-out donor to Anthony Weiner? Whoever got one-on-one with Trump would win because he was an open sewer of immorality and Republicans were the "Character Counts" party. Those of us who voiced this opinion were allowing ourselves to think that the Republican Party we wanted to exist actually did. It's not that we were stupid, but we were foolish. At least I was. If I look back on my years in politics, the long-standing hypocrisy of the Republican Party should have been obvious. I should have known better because I was there.

The first large, heavily funded conservative political action committee was called the National Conservative Political Action Committee (NCPAC, pronounced *nic*-pac). It was started in the mid-1970s with a mission to take advantage of a 1976 Supreme Court ruling that opened the door to independent groups' spending large sums of money on federal races. This was a way to circumvent the individual contribution limits on all federal races. I had never heard of NCPAC when I got a call from a Republican pollster named Arthur Finkelstein, asking me if I would like to make some ads for NCPAC. This was in 1982, when I had worked on a few winning campaigns. I had never heard of Arthur Finkelstein either, but he was the NCPAC pollster and a driving force behind conservatives like Jesse Helms. In retrospect, I'd like to say this troubled me, but the truth is that I was happy anyone wanted to hire me and I eagerly said yes.

Arthur was brilliant, darkly funny, deeply eccentric, and one of the more compelling characters I ever came across in politics. He was also gay and later moved to Massachusetts to avail himself of the LGBT rights that Governor Bill Weld helped pass. Arthur was a fierce defender of Jesse Helms, and when I once tried to raise the obvious contradictions of Helms's homophobia and Arthur's own sexual orientation, he actually burst out laughing. "Kid," he said, "all we do is elect them. After that they're on their own." Then he got more serious. "Your dad is a lawyer, right?" I said he was. "Do lawyers take on clients they don't agree with? Try to give them the best defense possible? Of course they do. That's how the whole legal system works. Everybody is entitled to a defense. Criminal defense lawyers don't even want to know if their guy is innocent. So if it's good enough for lawyers, why not for us?" I remember being flattered that he would include me in the "us," as though I had been admitted to some secret society of political consultants when I really was just a guy stumbling around in politics.

The head of NCPAC was Terry Dolan. He was also gay and later died of AIDS. As far as I could tell, NCPAC was a gay organization dedicated to electing the most conservative and antigay politicians in America. A typical NCPAC fund-raising letter would include sections like "Our nation's moral fiber is being weakened by the growing homosexual movement and the fanatical ERA pushers (many of whom publicly brag they are lesbians)."[7] They worked closely with Jerry Falwell, whose Moral Majority sponsored the Family Protection Act introduced in 1979 by two of NCPAC's favorite senators, Nevada's Paul Laxalt (chairman of the Reagan presidential campaign) and Iowa's Roger Jepsen. The major focus of the legislation was a broad attack on women, from limiting contraception to banning abortion and reaffirming the rightful place of women to be in the home. But it also was explicitly an attack on the sexual orientation of the leaders of NCPAC who so fervently advocated the election of the sponsors. The bill would cut off all federal funding for any organization "advocating, promoting, or suggesting homosexuality, male or female, as a life style."[8]

All of this should have bothered me, but I honestly didn't think about it much. I never worked directly for Jesse Helms or any candidate that I didn't like. I helped elect pro-choice and pro-gay-rights governors like Bill Weld of Massachusetts and Tom Ridge of Pennsylvania. I made ads for Senator Dan Coats of Indiana, who was named Head Start Man of the Year in 1991. Later, when I saw *Angels in America*, the Roy

Cohn character resonated as the perfect encapsulation of the strange denial of the gay extreme right. Here is how he described himself:

> I don't want you to be impressed. I want you to understand. This is not sophistry. And this is not hypocrisy. This is reality. I have sex with men. But unlike nearly every other man of whom this is true, I bring the guy I'm screwing to the White House and President Reagan smiles at us and shakes his hand. Because *what* I am is defined entirely by *who* I am. Roy Cohn is not a homosexual. Roy Cohn is a heterosexual man, Henry, who fucks around with guys.[9]

The "heterosexual man, Henry, who fucks around with guys" pretty much sums up the contradiction of the Christian right as a force in Republican politics. They claim to represent evangelicals when they actually mean they represent white evangelicals. Like referring to "working-class voters" when describing white working-class voters, they aim to disenfranchise black voters from the political discussion. When leaders of today's Christian right declare that Donald Trump's election is a sign from God, they are following in a tradition that dates from the Crusades and is embraced by the Ku Klux Klan: "It is God's will." In *God and Donald Trump*, the author Stephen Strang explains how Trump's election was a fulfillment of prophecy:

> I have also spoken with several religious leaders identified as modern-day prophets. Many of these individuals

prophesied well before the election that God was raising up Donald Trump like the ancient Persian king Cyrus the Great, a pagan chosen by God for a purpose only he could accomplish. The prophets told me they had certain knowledge that Trump would win. And, lo and behold, he did.[10]

It is a strange phenomenon of Republican politics that candidates are quick to announce that God would like them to win. Ted Cruz's father gave a detailed description of how God intervened:

My son Ted and his family spent six months in prayer seeking God's will for this decision. But the day the final green light came on, the whole family was together. It was a Sunday. We were all at his church, First Baptist Church in Houston, including his senior staff. After the church service, we all gathered at the pastor's office. We were on our knees for two hours seeking God's will. At the end of that time, a word came through his wife, Heidi. And the word came, just saying, "Seek God's face, not God's hand." And I'll tell you, it was as if there was a cloud of the Holy Spirit filling that place. Some of us were weeping, and Ted just looked up and said, "Lord, here am I, use me. I surrender to you, whatever you want." And he felt that was a green light to move forward.[11]

Rick Perry told a fund-raising crowd before he announced, "At 27 years old, I knew that I had been called to the ministry. I've just always been really stunned by how big a pulpit I was gonna have. I still am. I truly believe with all my heart that God has put me in this place at this time to do his will."[12]

In case you're thinking you didn't know that Rick Perry was a minister, he isn't. The "ministry" he was called to was the Texas House of Representatives, which has seldom been confused with a church. As Texas governor, Perry announced a three-day prayer to end a long drought. The proclamation read,

WHEREAS, throughout our history, both as a state and as individuals, Texans have been strengthened, assured and lifted up through prayer; it seems right and fitting that the people of Texas should join together in prayer to humbly seek an end to this devastating drought and these dangerous wildfires;

Now, therefore, I, Rick Perry, Governor of Texas, under the authority vested in me by the Constitution and Statutes of the State of Texas, do hereby proclaim the three-day period from Friday, April 22, 2011, to Sunday, April 24, 2011, as Days of Prayer for Rain in the State of Texas.[13]

Perry didn't win the presidential election, and it was 168 days after the Days of Prayer before it rained in Texas. In a Bush campaign meeting in 2000, when we had lousy polling numbers, a young staffer said that she knew God wouldn't let us lose. To which Matthew Dowd, who was coordinating the polling, gently said, "I'm not sure God is following the tracking." Now whenever I hear the loonies on the right asserting that God wanted Trump to win, I always wonder why it didn't occur to them that if God really was involved, he probably could have won the popular vote for Trump. And done it without the Russians' helping.

Eighty-one percent of evangelicals supported Trump in 2016, a number slightly higher than those of George W. Bush, who was a born-again Christian, and Mitt Romney, a devout Mormon whose values and life choices could not be more different from Donald Trump's.[14] I worked for both Bush and Romney, have spent a great deal of time with both, seen them in moments of intense pressure, crushing disappointment, in victory and defeat. I've been with them when they were exhausted and frayed, forced to deal with the inevitable mishaps and mistakes of a presidential campaign. I've been with them on buses that broke down, planes that were grounded, when microphones didn't work and angry supporters wanted to lecture them on everything they were doing wrong. I've seen them with their families and how they light up around kids. These are men whose politics you might abhor, but it was difficult not to recognize they were decent men who tried to live their lives by a set of values that represented the best of our society. Both were born into great privilege and remained humble. Neither of these men could win a primary for president in the current Republican Party. Decency, kindness, humility, compassion—all touchstones of a Christian faith—have no value in today's Republican Party. All his life, Donald Trump has believed these to be weaknesses, and now that is the view of the party he leads. Peter Wehner was a Bush speechwriter and evangelical Christian who now writes for *The New York Times.* He was an early and eloquent voice against Donald Trump, declaring early on he would never support him. A year into the Trump presidency, after Trump had led the GOP to endorse Roy Moore in Alabama, Wehner wrote, in a piece for *The New York Times* titled "Why I Can No Longer Call Myself an Evangelical Republican,"

I hoped the Trump era would be seen as an aberration and made less ugly by those who might have influence over the president. That hasn't happened. Rather than Republicans and people of faith checking his most unappealing sides, the president is dragging down virtually everyone within his orbit.[15]

My friend Rick Wilson, another early Trump critic and a longtime Republican consultant, wrote a book called *Everything Trump Touches Dies.*[16] Rick understood that Trump will always put himself before anyone and any value and that a lifetime of scams, frauds, scandals, and lies has proven that whoever associates with Trump is discredited. So it is with evangelicals. They cannot pretend, as they might have been able to in 2016, that Donald Trump would change and "grow into" the office, in an oft-used phrase that never made any sense. They know the man they are supporting for reelection wrote hush-money checks while in the Oval Office to the porn star he had sex with ten days after his youngest son was born. Michael Gerson, another Bush speechwriter and evangelical, sums up what the marriage of Trump and evangelicals has wrought:

It is remarkable to hear religious leaders defend profanity, ridicule, and cruelty as hallmarks of authenticity and dismiss decency as a dead language. Whatever Trump's policy legacy ends up being, his presidency has been a disaster in the realm of norms. It has coarsened our culture, given permission for bullying, complicated the moral formation of children, undermined standards of public integrity, and encouraged cynicism about the political enterprise. Falwell, Graham, and others are providing religious cover for moral squalor—winking at trashy behavior and encouraging the unraveling of social restraints. Instead of defending their convictions, they are providing preemptive absolution for their political favorites. And this, even by purely political standards, undermines the causes they embrace.[17]

There is usefulness in the sad squalor of watching so-called Christian leaders lead their flocks into supporting the least religious president in American history. When these same leaders were supporting Republicans like George W. Bush and Mitt Romney, it made it easier for them to assert they were fighting for a greater good for civil society. But anger and racism and fear of the future have always lurked beneath the surface of the Christian right, like a menacing shark disturbing a calm ocean. Now they are in the open, and we need no longer pretend that those who support bad men like Roy Moore and Donald Trump are remotely motivated by love of neighbor or charity or compassion. The fear of a changing world is now validated and given legitimacy at the highest levels. They are free now to be openly what they felt obligated to mask. They can now admit it was all a lie.

3

THE LONG CON

The Republican Congress now represents a party with
very few significant defining principles other than the
promotion of the president's impulses at that moment.
—Republican former senator
Judd Gregg of New Hampshire[1]

The day I sat down to write this chapter, *The New York Times* broke the story that Donald Trump for over a decade had managed to lose more money than any other American and, in some years, twice as much as any other American. This is the man Republicans chose because of his business smarts and success:

And so, year after year, Mr. Trump appears to have lost more money than nearly any other individual taxpayer, according to the I.R.S. information on high earners—a publicly available database with taxpayers' identifying details removed. Indeed, in 1990 and 1991, his core businesses lost more than $250 million each year—more than double those of the nearest taxpayers in the sampling for those years.[2]

The story was the perfect corollary to the larger narrative of the Republican Party. Trump was running a scam on investors, and the Republican Party has been running a similar scam on voters. Trump claims to be a great businessman who was wildly successful, while in fact he was one of the greatest failures in modern American business history. The Republican Party claims to be a party that understands the need to run government efficiently, managing debt and balancing a budget. In truth the modern Republican Party is the equivalent of Donald Trump: addicted to debt and selling a false image of success. The 2016 National Republican Party Platform attacked the Obama administration for a "huge increase in the national debt":

Reducing the Federal Debt

Our national debt is a burden on our economy and families. The huge increase in the national debt demanded by and incurred during the current Administration has placed a significant burden on future generations. We must impose firm caps on future debt, accelerate the repayment of the trillions we now owe in order to reaffirm our principles of responsible and limited government, and remove the burdens we are placing on future generations.

A strong economy is one key to debt reduction, but spending restraint is a necessary component that must be vigorously pursued.[3]

The 2012 National Republican Party Platform was unequivocal in its depiction of the destructive forces of national debt:

Unless we take dramatic action now, young Americans and their children will inherit an unprecedented legacy of enormous and unsustainable debt, with the interest alone consuming an ever-increasing portion of the country's wealth. The specter of national bankruptcy that now hangs over much of Europe is a warning to us as well. Over the last three and a half years, while cutting the defense budget, the current Administration has added an additional $5.3 trillion to the national debt— now approximately $16 trillion, the largest amount in U.S. history.[4]

So what happened when the Republican Party, in a shocking upset, won control of all three chambers of government for the first time since 2007? The federal debt skyrocketed. In less than two and a half years, the debt increased at record levels, from $20 trillion to $22 trillion.[5] All but six months of that period was under the Republican-controlled White House, House of Representatives, and Senate.

When he ran for president, Donald Trump promised to balance the budget in eight years. In an interview with *The Washington Post*'s Bob Woodward, Trump relied upon his usual jumbled view of trade to explain how he would get it done:

We're not a rich country. We're a debtor nation. We've got to get rid of—I talked about bubble. We've got to get rid of the $19 trillion in debt.

BW: How long would that take?

DT: I think I could do it fairly quickly, because of the fact the numbers—

BW: What's fairly quickly?

DT: Well, I would say over a period of eight years. And I'll tell you why.

BW: Would you ever be open to tax increases as part of that, to solve the problem?

DT: I don't think I'll need to. The power is trade. Our deals are so bad.

BW: That would be $2 trillion a year.

DT: No, but I'm renegotiating all of our deals, Bob. The big trade deals that we're doing so badly on. With China, $505 billion this year in trade. We're losing with everybody.[6]

In a typical dog's breakfast of facts, Trump takes a number close to the total trade deficit of the United States in 2016 and blames it on China. Instead of decreasing national debt the $2 trillion a year promised, he increased it $2 trillion in a little over two years. Now, not surprisingly, the national debt has disappeared from Trump's standard speeches and was not mentioned in his 2018 or 2019 State of the Union speeches. To get a sense of just how far this is from the beating heart of a central tenet of conservatism and what it means to be a Republican, here's Paul Ryan on national debt in his acceptance speech at the 2012 Republican National Convention:

In this generation, a defining responsibility of government is to steer our nation clear of a debt crisis while there is still time. Back in 2008, candidate Obama called a $10 trillion national debt "unpatriotic"—serious talk from what looked to be a serious reformer.

Yet by his own decisions, President Obama has added more debt than any other president before him, and more than all the troubled governments of Europe combined. One president, one term, $5 trillion in new debt.

So here we are, $16 trillion in debt and still he does nothing. In Europe, massive debts have put entire governments at risk of collapse, and still he does nothing. And all we have heard from this president and his team are attacks on anyone who dares to point out the obvious.

They have no answer to this simple reality: We need to stop spending money we don't have.[7]

During Paul Ryan's speakership, there was no 9/11 or Great Recession to place upward pressure on the deficit. Republicans had promised for decades to control spending, and when given a chance, they decided it was easier to just spend more. But blaming Speaker Ryan for this deficit disaster is too easy. Had there been any remote desire or will in either party to do what it takes to cut the deficit, Ryan would have happily pushed that agenda. What happened under Ryan isn't so much about him as about exposing the fundamental falsehood that Republicans ever cared about the deficit. The history of the national debt is like all history: it varies greatly by authorship. But a few basic facts are indisputable: in the post–World War II era, Republican presidents have contributed far more to the deficit than Democrats. As Steve Clemons wrote in *The Atlantic,* when it comes to reducing the debt, "the big winner is Harry Truman, followed by Bill Clinton. Eisenhower is next, followed by Johnson and Nixon, Kennedy, and finally Jimmy Carter. All of these presidents reduced debt as a percent of

GDP."[8] The great modern-era success story is Bill Clinton. In his January 1998 State of the Union address, Clinton was accurately able to claim,

> When I took office, the deficit for 1998 was projected to be $357 billion and heading higher. This year, our deficit is projected to be $10 billion and heading lower. For three decades, six Presidents have come before you to warn of the damage deficits pose to our nation. Tonight I come before you to announce that the federal deficit, once so incomprehensibly large that it had 11 zeros, will be, simply, zero. I will submit to Congress for 1999 the first balanced budget in 30 years.[9]

What is most remarkable—and telling—about the Clinton success on the deficit is the furious degree that he was opposed by Republicans. Not one Republican voted for his 1993 budget package that combined tax increases and spending cuts. In 1994, I and just about every other Republican political consultant made ads attacking the Clinton tax increases and predicting economic disaster unless repealed. The Republican predictions of economic calamity following the Clinton administration were dire. Speaker Newt Gingrich:

> We have all too many people in the Democratic administration who are talking about bigger Government, bigger bureaucracy, more programs, and higher taxes. I believe that that will in fact kill the current recovery and put us back in a recession. It might take 1½ or 2 years, but it will happen.[10]

The former Reagan White House staffer and future chairman of the Securities and Exchange Commission Christopher Cox was lurid in his pronouncement of imminent doom: "This is really the Dr. Kevorkian plan for our economy. It will kill jobs, kill businesses, and yes, kill even the higher tax revenues that these suicidal tax increasers hope to gain."[11]

The Republican ads and message worked beautifully, and Republicans gained fifty-four seats in the House and eight Senate seats, giving Republicans control of Congress for the first time since 1952. This was the "Contract with America" election billed as the "Republican Revolution." As a Republican consultant, it was one of those cycles in which you wanted to do a ton of races because everyone was likely to win. My firm won every campaign we did that year, fourteen statewide races. I was never burdened by the notion that I was working for a political party that was fundamentally hypocritical on the deficit and economy and one that would proceed to impeach Bill Clinton for lying about sex under the leadership of Speaker Newt Gingrich, who was having an affair with a former House intern himself. The point of politics, as far as I could see, was to win, and when you were winning, what could possibly be wrong?

Instead of killing the economy as Republicans predicted, the Clinton economic plan helped launch one of the longest periods of economic growth in U.S. history and helped create twenty-three million new jobs. Incomes rose; poverty fell. The only period of greater growth was the post–economic crash under the Obama years.[12] (Yeah, that sort of drives Republicans crazy too.) But talk to most Republicans who were part of the Clinton era, and they will insist it was the

Republican Congress that guided the economy to one of the greatest economic success stories in U.S. history. Of course had the economy tanked, they would have blamed Clinton and claimed their predictions were accurate. In retrospect, the Clinton presidency adhered to the values espoused for decades by Republicans far more than the Trump years. Clinton had the first budget surpluses since 1969. When he took office, the ratio of the national debt to gross national product was 47.7 percent. It fell to 33.6 percent. This skyrocketed to over 100 percent during the Obama administration, in part because of stimulus spending to dig the country out of the Great Recession. In the Republican years of Trump, it has only grown worse. Clinton also signed NAFTA back when Republicans insisted they were for free trade. But supporting free trade was just another quaint marketing slogan that was useful until it was more convenient to fall in love with the Trump tariffs.

Everybody loves to spend more money, particularly when it's seen as someone else's money. It's not a uniquely Republican addiction, but the blame falls to Republicans for being a breathtaking combination of hypocritical and unaware. Ask most white Republicans in "red" states about government's spending too much, and they will rail against welfare and probably throw in a little California hating because, well, it's California and all kinds of satanic evils are being perpetuated in that state Donald Trump calls a "disaster."[13] For all their bluster about the federal government and states' rights, the most conservative states in the country are far and away the most dependent on federal aid.

Like my native Mississippi. For every dollar Mississippians pay in federal income tax, the state receives just over $3 back from the federal government. More than 40 percent of Mississippi's entire budget comes from Washington. Who pays for that? Those evil states like California and New York, where the good citizens pay a dollar in taxes and get less back from the government. Every time a New Yorker or Californian goes to work, he or she is helping build roads, hospitals, and schools in Mississippi. Trump won West Virginia by more than forty points. For every dollar a West Virginian pays in taxes, the state gets more than $2 back.[14] Does anybody really think the elected officials from those states are going to get serious about cutting the federal budget? It's true of Democrats and Republicans, but in contemporary America those poor states are overwhelmingly Republican.

In 2014, the Mississippi Republican senator Thad Cochran was up for reelection. He was seventy-six and had first been elected in 1978, the year I made my first political ads for his former chief of staff Jon Hinson. Cochran was challenged in the primary by a forty-three-year-old state senator named Chris McDaniel. The McDaniel campaign was a product of the post–*Citizens United* Supreme Court campaign financing ruling world. As an obscure state senator who had never run statewide before, he had little base of support in Mississippi and no established fund-raising network. Before *Citizens United* cleared the way for outside groups to spend unlimited money supporting a candidate, a small-time state senator would not have had a chance against a well-funded, powerful U.S. senator who was well liked in the state. But a few powerful conservative groups in Washington targeted Cochran, long a member of the Senate Appropriations Committee, as a perfect example of pork barrel spending, a senator who had used his influence and seniority to increase spending and steer as much as possible to Mississippi. These groups encouraged McDaniel to run and poured more than $7 million into defeating Cochran, attacking him for wasteful spending. In his own campaign, McDaniel raised a fraction of that amount, leading the former Mississippi governor (and longtime client of mine) Haley Barbour to call our McDaniel campaign a front for "a bunch of out-of-state political gunslingers who have crowned themselves as the leaders of Tea Party Republicanism."[15]

The outside groups saw McDaniel as a good bet based on their polling that showed Republican voters in Mississippi overwhelmingly favored cutting federal spending. In the Cochran campaign, we had the same numbers. But I never believed it. And if it was accurate, Cochran had no chance. So we decided to throw out the polling and run a very traditional message that Thad Cochran could deliver more for Mississippi. Instead of trying to convince voters that Cochran really wanted to cut government spending, we focused on the specific benefits he had delivered for Mississippi through federal funding. Instead of running against "earmarked" spending, we bragged about all the bacon Cochran had brought home to the poorest state in the nation. From schools to roads to military installations to shipbuilding on the Gulf Coast to grants for local law enforcement, we made ads with specific examples of why Mississippians were better off with a powerful senator who would fight for every dollar. About 40 percent of Mississippi's state budget is funded by the federal government, as high as any state in the country.

It was a brutal race. After my firm was hired, I went down for a few days to help out and ended up spending six weeks. While the outside groups were focused on attacking Cochran for spending, McDaniel was running as racist a campaign as I'd seen in Mississippi since the 1970s, including ads that carefully focused on the part of the state flag that was a near replica of the Confederate battle flag. In Mississippi a candidate must win a primary with at least 50 percent, or the top two go into a runoff election three weeks later. The race was so close between Cochran and McDaniel that the 1.6 percent of votes cast for an obscure candidate threw the race into a runoff. Starting with his first run for Congress in the early 1970s, Cochran had always refused to play to Mississippi's dark side, never using the dog-whistle rhetoric that was standard for white politicians. He was a gentle, kind man whose parents had been schoolteachers and stressed racial tolerance. More than any other white Republican Mississippi politician of the era, Cochran had developed a reservoir of goodwill with the African American community, including the endorsement of Charles Evers, brother of the slain civil rights advocate Medgar Evers. In the runoff election, we made a concentrated effort to bring African American voters into the primary. It was a matter not really of getting new voters for Cochran but of trying to identify and motivate those who had voted for him in previous elections. Much of the federal aid Cochran had brought to Mississippi had helped those most disadvantaged economically, and the contrast with

McDaniel, who was promising deep cuts, played well with these voters.

Few gave Cochran a chance in the runoff election, the thinking being that if you have been a senator since 1978 and can't persuade enough voters to push you over 50 percent in a primary, what are you going to do or say in the next three weeks that you hadn't done or said in the last forty years? But Cochran won by more than seven thousand votes. Hardly a landslide, but as Chris Cillizza of *The Washington Post* put it, the race was "like watching someone pitch a political perfect game; you'll not see a victory like this one any time soon." Cillizza correctly understood the counterintuitive direction we had taken the campaign:

> Look at Cochran's message on TV in the closing days of the race. It's a Republican message circa 2004: I have tons of seniority in the Senate and that means good things for the state. Vote me out and you can kiss all of that goodbye. (Hell, he brought Arizona Sen. John McCain in to campaign for him in the final days of the contest!) There is absolutely no evidence—before this victory—that a longtime incumbent running on being, well, a longtime incumbent could win in the modern day Republican party. And especially not in a runoff! It did in this case.[16]

After his loss, Chris McDaniel refused to concede and blasted Cochran for winning with "Democratic" voters. In Mississippi there is no party registration—"party is a state of mind" is the classic description—so what McDaniel was really saying was that Cochran had won with black votes. While Cochran did increase his support with blacks in the runoff, it's doubtful it made up the seven thousand plus vote margin. But the race did illustrate the deeply contradictory attitude of conservatives toward spending. At the end of the day, Mississippi Republicans, as conservative a bunch of voters as you will find in America, came down on the side of supporting a man who could help deliver more dollars to their state. And had no problem still insisting that federal spending was out of control. In my thirty-plus years of working in Republican campaigns, I can't think of a single instance where the message of cutting spending really moved numbers toward a Republican. Attacking a Democrat for wasteful spending—the "bridge to nowhere" was the classic case—can work, but like in the Cochran-McDaniel race there seems little upside to promising to cut specific spending that benefits a constituency. If the deficit is ever going to be cut, Republicans (and Democrats) have to be willing to take steps that are not immediately popular, and that includes real spending cuts combined with "revenue enhancements," which is what tax increases are called when no one wants to admit they are tax increases.

In a Washington increasingly divided by ideology, one of the few places where right meets left is the concurrence that the vast majority of farm subsidies are a wasteful scam. The left-leaning Environmental Working Group and the Union of Concerned Scientists praised the conservative Heritage Foundation, which opposes gun control and considers the Democratic Green New Deal a vast left-wing conspiracy, for its call to end farm subsidies. After a withering Heritage report deconstructing the need for farm subsidies, the Environmental Working Group agreed with Heritage: "Today's report confirms how our so-called farm safety net has strayed from its original purpose—to help farmers weather the ups and [downs in] agriculture, not to guarantee a level income that is well above the income of the average American household."[17] The Union of Concerned Scientists agreed:

> The Heritage report highlights many ill effects of the current federal farm subsidy system. We absolutely must continue to support farmers, particularly when they need it most, but that support shouldn't come at the cost of incentivizing certain crops and practices over others, exacerbating land access issues, or disproportionately supporting the largest and wealthiest farm businesses.[18]

Farmers have good years and bad years—like every other business—but the median income of farm households is consistently higher than the median income of nonfarm households. The average American household has a net worth of $82,600, versus $827,000 for farm households.[19] About half of the billions in farm subsidies go to farmers with household income over $150,000. If Republicans—or Democrats—were remotely serious about cutting the deficit, wouldn't it be a logical step to cut out what amounts to farming welfare for rich farmers?

In a piece called "The Farm Bill Is Everything That's Wrong with Congress," Alex Shephard wrote in *The New Republic,*

> The Farm Bill was initially conceived as a response to the Dust Bowl and the Great Depression, an effort to provide fair prices for both consumers and farmers, access to quality food, and protection for natural resources. It wasn't until 1965 when the funding for the Supplemental Nutrition Assistance Program (SNAP, aka food stamps) and efforts to regulate and support commodity prices were combined into a single omnibus bill—this was because neither was able to pass on its own, a situation that has grown only more dire under this polarized Congress.[20]

The linking of farm subsidies and food stamps makes sense if anyone thinks the government has equal obligation to help wealthy farmers and poor Americans. In a sane world, aid would be need-driven with any subsidies going to farmers in need just as food stamps are need-based. But the conglomerate that is known as the farm lobby fights every effort to means-test farm subsidies. Meanwhile, Republicans continue to push to make it increasingly difficult to qualify for food stamps. The hypocrisy is not lost on some in the agricultural community. In a *Washington Post* interview, the former USDA chief economist Joe Glauber acknowledged the hypocrisy of the farm lobby taking a stand against income testing for eligibility for farm subsidies, while "you have a knockdown drag-out over whether you'll give SNAP payments to someone earning $26,000 instead of $25,000. Give me a break."[21]

As the magazine *The American Conservative* notes, "Agricultural subsidies are one of the most important examples of corporate welfare—money handed out to businesses based on political connections."[22] There's a language war here that Republicans have been winning for decades. "Welfare" is what the poor get because they are, well, poor, and being poor is a choice because in America anyone can succeed. Or something close to that. But "grants," "tax breaks," and "incentives" are the language businesses use to describe the corporate welfare they demand in exchange for doing what they usually have to do or want to do anyway, like build a new data center or factory or, in the case of sports, a new stadium. Often the real description should be corporate blackmail. Big business has mastered the art of pitting one state against another state in a sort of eBay bidding war in which politicians desperate to claim they have "created" some mythical number of new jobs bid against each other using taxpayer dollars.

A watchdog organization called Good Jobs First analyzed the subsidies received by high-tech giants. As reported in the San Jose *Mercury News,*

> Tesla, valued by market capitalization at $54 billion, led the way by far, with $3.5 billion in public-money subsidies since 2007. Google's parent Alphabet, market cap $762 billion, has received $766 million since 2000, with most of the subsidies coming since 2011. Apple, market cap $894 billion, has racked up $693 million in subsidies since 2009. Facebook, market cap $549 billion, has reaped $333 million since 2010. In Nevada subsidies

to Tesla cost local governments $68.7 million in 2016, with a school district near Reno losing $36.7 million in revenue "solely to Tesla subsidies."[23]

Then there's the whole world of sports madness where billionaire owners somehow manage to get regular taxpayers to underwrite the cost of new stadiums that are basically a license to print money for the monopoly-protected owners. Arthur Blank, who co-founded Home Depot and owns the Atlanta Falcons, managed to get more than $700 million in tax breaks and subsidies to build his new sports palace. Some owners do even better, getting more in breaks than the cost of a stadium.[24] Is it fair to lay the insanity of middle-class taxpayers' subsidizing billionaires at the feet of the Republican Party? At any given game, Arthur Blank's suite at the Falcons' new stadium will be graced with happy politicians from both parties who feel so special they are invited to the inner sanctum of the billionaire their constituents worked hard to support. But if Republicans were serious about being the party of fiscal responsibility, they would combine any efforts to cut entitlements with a real push to end corporate welfare of all kinds, on the state or federal level. For decades on the center right, there have been endless amounts of self-serious declarations on the need to change the "culture" of welfare, the "culture" of dependency. All of that had a net positive impact, focusing attention on examples of the failures of the best intentions of the Great Society years. Yes, some of it was ill-disguised racist tripe that blamed the poor for being poor. But the welfare system did need reform, as Bill

Clinton famously declared in his 1992 campaign pitch to "end welfare as we know it." Where is the equivalent when it comes to corporate welfare? Republicans have largely been silent and let the left like Bernie Sanders define the outrage.

How about cutting the defense budget? Of the so-called discretionary spending—that is, the part of the budget that is not increasing on automatic formulas—around 50 percent goes to the military budget. When's the last time you heard a Republican talking about cutting the military? Republicans ridiculed President Obama and Senator Bernie Sanders for claiming that the United States spends more on the military than the next twelve countries combined. Well, it's true—or mostly true, depending on the year. Sometimes it has dipped as low as only the next eight or ten countries. The next ten would include China, Russia, Saudi Arabia, India, France, the U.K., Germany, Italy, and Japan.[25] Any serious attempt to balance the budget by necessity would include defense cuts, but Republicans have decided there is a direct correlation between the size of a patriotic heart and the size of the defense budget. This patriotism-equals-defense-spending is now so common with Republicans that it's difficult to remember when it was otherwise. I made ads attacking John Kerry for supporting defense cuts. I made ads attacking Bill Clinton for reducing defense spending. One of the great modern political commercials is the Bush 1988 ad showing Michael Dukakis in a tank wearing a helmet that made him look like the Snoopy character, with a voice-over detailing the defense cuts he proposed. I didn't make that ad—Roger Ailes's team of ad makers did—but I loved it and thought it was brilliant. So did a lot of other people. For those voters who thought national defense was a key issue, Bush crushed Dukakis.

But have we forgotten? President Eisenhower cut defense spending by 27 percent after the Korean War. President Nixon cut the budget by 29 percent from the peak of the Vietnam War. There was a stretch of eleven years, from 1987 to 1998, in which Presidents Reagan, Bush, and Clinton used the end of the cold war to control defense spending.[26] Donald Trump is the most isolationist president since Herbert Hoover, attacking NATO and ridiculing America's need to support allies. But he still supports increased military spending and, in a typically boastful lie, claims that when he became president, the military was running out of ammunition. In the end, Americans get the worst of both worlds. Our taxes pay for an ever-increasing military budget, while our respect in the world has plummeted with Trump as a leader. In the sandbox of Donald Trump's mind, spending more on defense proves he's a tough guy, while working with allies proves he's weak.

The center-right think tank American Enterprise Institute summed up well the Republican pattern of using the deficit and fiscal restraint as a weapon to hit Democrats:

> The GOP is just as culpable as Democrats for the dismal fiscal outlook because the party engages in excessive and simplistic bombast on the budget when it is out of power and then wastes its time on distractions when it has the opportunity to make progress with incremental reforms.

In 2017, the Trump administration called for deep cuts in domestic appropriations that were intended to

create the perception of fiscal restraint. The Republican-
controlled Congress all but ignored the proposed cuts.
In the end, Republicans worked with Democrats to raise
appropriations for defense and non-defense accounts by
a combined $300 billion over two years. This spending
isn't why the government is awash in debt, but the process by which it came about is emblematic of Republican
ineptitude on fiscal policy.[27]

Most great governmental disasters are rooted in some
large, fundamental misconception, which in politics is usually
just another word for lie. The subprime mortgage meltdown
was predicated upon the government's deception that housing
prices could only continue to rise. In the category of good
intentions gone bad, conservatives accelerated the crisis by
pushing the concept of an "ownership society" that would
help alleviate poverty as well as the idea that government
should lower barriers to home ownership whenever possible.
The second Iraq war was driven by the terribly wrong conviction that Iraq had weapons of mass destruction. (I've never
bought the idea that this was a deliberate lie, if only because
the one thing you can say about politicians like Tony Blair and
George W. Bush is that they do not like to be proven wrong,
and if they believed no weapons of mass destruction would be
found, they would not have set themselves up for an inevitable
humiliation. But that's another book.) The 9/11 attacks were
rooted in the false sense of security the government fostered
and a failure to imagine worst-case scenarios of terrorism.
The massive breakdown of disaster relief with Hurricane

Katrina was rooted in state and local governmental agencies' and elected officials' lying to the public for decades. Read the Brookings Institution's list "Government's Most Visible Failures, 2001–2014"; it is a heartbreaking accumulation of avoidable tragedies and misery in just that short period, almost all rooted in some large, fundamental miscalculation.[28]

So it is with the Republican Party's modern love affair with tax cuts. In the Republican presidential primary of 1980, George H. W. Bush called the Reagan tax plan "voodoo economics," which fit perfectly the writer Michael Kinsley's definition that "a gaffe is when a politician tells the truth—some obvious truth he isn't supposed to say."[29] Bush summed up the utterly nutty idea that it was possible to cut taxes and increase spending without adding to the deficit. When Reagan took office, the national debt was $934 billion; when he left, it was $2.7 trillion. It isn't as if the outcome were some great surprise brought on by unforeseen events. Just two and a half years into the first Reagan administration, *The New York Times* analyzed the successes and failures of "Reaganomics," and it was clear then that deficits were a critical problem:

> Even prominent Republican economists see ominous portents in the deficits. "The biggest mistake so far," said Rudolph G. Penner, who was the chief economist in the Ford Administration's budget office, "was to urge this tremendous cut in taxes without reducing spending sufficiently. That is a major mistake that will have profound long run costs."

The *Times* captured the concept that tax cuts were more than an economic tool to Reagan and many of his administration:

> Reaganomics, however, is something more than a theory of managing a national economy. To the President in particular, it is something spiritual. The changes in the tax laws that he sponsored, such as the reductions of rates in all income brackets and the resulting reduction of capital gains taxes, do indeed benefit the rich far more than the poor. But when asked at his news conference this week whether the often-repeated charge that his policies boiled down to economics for the rich, the President said: "The Rich Don't Need My Help."
>
> "No, the rich don't need my help, and I'm not doing things to help the rich. I think I'm doing things to help all the people. But what I want to see above all is that this country remains a country where someone can always get rich. That's the thing that we have, and that's the thing that must be preserved."[30]

For many in the Reagan administration, this "spiritual" attachment to tax cuts was connected to a cultlike devotion to the libertarian author Ayn Rand, which is odd in that Ayn Rand hated Ronald Reagan. In *Goddess of the Market: Ayn Rand and the American Right,* Jennifer Burns described how Rand toward the end of her life "had one last word of warning to issue. Referring to the upcoming Republican primaries she wrote, 'I urge you, as emphatically as I can, not to support the candidacy of Ronald Reagan.' Reagan was a conservative in 'the worst sense of the word,' she told her readers."[31] But for many in the Reagan circle, that their love of Ayn Rand was unrequited did not preclude their emotional attachment to her vision of strong men fighting against the burdensome yoke of collectivism and government oppression. Ayn Rand defined her beliefs in the context of her native Russia gone mad with Communism, but the Reagan crowd harnessed their inner John Galt to believe they had a moral duty to cut taxes, particularly for the wealthy, who were the most deserving because they were, well, wealthy and had proven themselves superior to those of lesser means. George Gilder, who is seen as one of the key architects of the Reagan economic plan, acknowledged that even though "Ayn Rand devoted much of her last public lecture, a speech at the Ford Hall Forum in Cambridge, Massachusetts, to a case against my ideas[,] I hugely admired Rand."[32]

A belief in the power of tax cuts is about as close as it can be to a definitional core belief that exists in the Republican Party. In campaign circles, it's assumed to be a given truth that Walter Mondale lost in 1984 when he said in his Democratic National Convention acceptance speech, "Let's tell the truth. Mr. Reagan will raise taxes, and so will I. He won't tell you. I just did." Reagan's response was clear: "I will propose no increase in personal income taxes and I will veto any tax bill that would raise personal income tax rates for working Americans or that would fail to make our tax system simpler or more fair."[33]

And it's assumed to be a given truth that George H. W.

Bush lost his 1992 reelection when he broke the pledge made in his 1988 convention acceptance speech: "Read my lips. No new taxes." A Clinton campaign ad featured video of Bush making the pledge, with an announcer declaring in ominous tones, "Then George Bush signed the second-biggest tax increase in American history." The Bush pledge repeated, and the announcer continued, "George Bush increased taxes on the middle class. Bush doubled the beer tax and increased the gas tax by 56 percent. Now George Bush wants to give a $108,000 tax break to millionaires. $108,000! Guess who's going to pay?"[34]

Both of these "truths" are probably false. Mondale didn't lose forty-nine states because he promised to raise taxes, and it was the larger negative impression of the Bush economy that had far more impact on helping Clinton win than a single broken promise. Clinton raised taxes and was reelected. In that campaign, I made ads for Senator Bob Dole attacking the Clinton tax increases. But the negative political impact of Clinton's tax increases, which hurt Democrats badly in the 1994 midterms, was nullified by the colossal stupidity of Newt Gingrich as Speaker of the House. First Gingrich shut down the government for five days when Bill Clinton refused to sign a bill that would have increased premiums on Medicare. It took Gingrich only five days to back down when it became obvious that raising premiums on Medicare sounded a lot like a tax increase on everyone over sixty-five and probably not the hill worth dying on. When it was over, Gingrich tried to blame the shutdown on the ill will created between him and Clinton after a trip to Israel for the funeral of Yitzhak Rabin when Gingrich was asked to exit Air Force One out of the rear doors. "This is petty," Gingrich said, according to *The Washington Post*. "[But] you land at Andrews [Air Force Base] and you've been on the plane for 25 hours and nobody has talked to you and they ask you to get off the plane by the back ramp. . . . You just wonder, where is their sense of manners? Where is their sense of courtesy?" The New York *Daily News* responded with a screaming front-page headline, " 'Cry Baby' Newt's Tantrum: He Closed Down the Government Because Clinton Made Him Sit at the Back of the Plane." The accompanying cartoon of Gingrich crying in a diaper and holding a bottle was a classic. It was during this shutdown, when the White House staff was pared down to basics and interns took over much of the routine of answering phones and staffing the West Wing, that Bill Clinton encountered Monica Lewinsky. So there's that unintended consequence.[35]

As if to prove he was capable of screwing up even more monumentally, Gingrich shut the government down again a couple of weeks later, this time for twenty-one days over Christmas. Why? *The Washington Post,* in its brief history of all government shutdowns, summed it up like this:

Why did it happen? Republican leaders demanded that the White House propose a seven-year budget plan that balanced when using the CBO's economic forecasts, rather than the OMB's, which were more optimistic. The plan Clinton proposed still produced a $115 billion deficit in seven years according to CBO numbers, even as the OMB estimated that it would balance the bud-

get by then. The dispute was not resolved before the
continuing resolution agreed to a month earlier . . .
expired.

If that all sounds technical and a stupid reason to ruin the
holiday seasons for millions, that's how most Americans also
saw it at the time. As the *Post* summed it up,

> What resolved it? Republicans caved, basically, and
> passed legislation to keep the government open. Clinton,
> in turn, submitted a budget plan that the CBO said bal-
> anced the budget within seven years.[36]

The political consequences of all this Gingrich-induced
Wagnerian drama were that the ads we made attacking Bill
Clinton for raising taxes were like trying to accuse someone
of a mild traffic violation when your own client was up for
war crimes in The Hague. Four years later, as part of the
team assembled for Governor George W. Bush's presidential
campaign, I helped make ads for him on taxes. One of our
first was called "Priorities":

> BUSH: I believe that government should do a few things
> and do them well. My top priorities will be to preserve
> Social Security and Medicare and to strengthen educa-
> tion and our military.
>
> I believe that once priorities have been funded we
> should pass money back to the taxpayers. That's what
> I've done in Texas. I signed the two largest tax cuts in our
> state's history. And we still have no personal income tax.

I believe we ought to cut tax rates to continue economic growth and to broaden prosperity.[37]

In the first debate, Gore opened with a call for a middle-class tax cut and, in terms almost unimaginable now, talked about not squandering the budget surplus. "And I will cut taxes for middle-class families. I believe it's important to resist the temptation to squander our surplus."[38] Nineteen years later with a national debt pushing $23 trillion and climbing hourly, the mere mention of "surplus" in a presidential debate is like reading H. G. Wells describe World War I as the "the war that will end war." It seems . . . quaint and bathed in the glow of lost innocence. Gore went on to attack Bush on taxes:

The priorities are just very different. For every new dollar that I propose for spending on health care, Governor Bush spends $3 for a tax cut for the wealthiest 1 percent. Now, for every dollar that I propose to spend on education, he spends $5 on a tax cut for the wealthiest 1 percent. Those are very clear differences.[39]

Bush defended his plan for an across-the-board tax cut:

The federal government should take no more than a third of anybody's check. But I also dropped the bottom rate from 15 percent to 10 percent. Because by far the vast majority of the help goes to people at the bottom end of the economic ladder. If you're a family of four in Massachusetts, making $50,000, you get a 50% cut in the federal income taxes you pay.[40]

This went on back and forth through the rest of the debate and the rest of the campaign. We made more ads on taxes. We loved them. But they never really moved numbers. The year 2000 was the sort of environment in which an incumbent vice president should have won easily: peace and prosperity, a budget surplus, consumer confidence at record highs on Election Day. But the one message that did work was the theme of "restoring honor and dignity to the White House."[41] Just as the 1992 race became about change, the one race President Bush—former VP, former head of CIA, former RNC chairman, former congressman—couldn't win against a young governor from Arkansas who had never served in Washington, the 2000 race became about character. And that was the one race Bill Clinton's VP couldn't easily win.

In his nomination acceptance speech at the 2000 Republican Convention, a beautiful piece of writing by Michael Gerson, Bush spoke to the issue that resonated most with voters:

> So when I put my hand on the Bible, I will swear to not only uphold the laws of our land, I will swear to uphold the honor and dignity of the office to which I have been elected, so help me God. . . . My fellow citizens, we can begin again. . . . After all of the shouting and all of the scandal, after all the bitterness and broken faith, we can begin again.[42]

The inability of the tax issue to persuade voters in the 2000 campaign was played out again in the next three presidential races. In the Romney campaign, jobs and the slow economic recovery from the Great Recession dominated the race. But none of our polling showed that voters believed tax cuts were the key to reducing unemployment. Most voters who were for Romney or open to voting for Romney supported tax cuts, but there was no intensity to the issue. Had President Obama been promising a major tax increase on middle-class voters, it would have had power as an issue, but that's like saying had one candidate declared he was pro-terrorism, there's a high likelihood terrorism would spike as an issue. But still the Republican Party continues to push tax cuts the same way the Roman Catholic Church uses incense for High Mass, as a comforting symbolism for believers that reminds them of their identity.

The same political reality is tied to the deficit, and the two are linked in a deadly embrace of a dangerous status quo. Being against "out-of-control federal spending," a phrase I must have used in a hundred ads, is a catechism of the Republican faith. But no one really believes in it any more than communicants believe they are actually eating and drinking the body and blood of Christ. It just makes the members of the Republican Church feel closer to their political God. In reality, the Republican Party isn't serious about deficit reduction, because politicians know their voters don't feel affected by the mind-boggling numbers and subsequently don't really care. Republicans are forced by their political DNA to be in favor of lower taxes, even though the fantasy of decreasing the deficit with tax cuts becomes ever more difficult to sustain. Any pretense that the Republican Party, if only given complete control of all three chambers of power, would focus on the deficit was just one of the myths shattered in the first two years of the Trump presidency. There is little energy to cut spending in the center of the center left in the Democratic Party, and the possibility that a Bill Clinton Democrat could emerge to restore some semblance of financial stability to the federal budget seems as fanciful as the notion a Republican would. The most likely scenario is that the deficit will continue to pile up until there is a financial crisis that forces the country to feel debt pain. Then the odds are that it will give renewed energy to a tax plan that greatly increases taxes on the wealthy.

This would be a fittingly ironic fate facing the so-called fiscal conservatives of the Republican Party. By pretending to care about an issue without the courage or will to act, they will have set in motion a scenario that is among their worst nightmares: an activated left with the moral authority to soak the rich with taxes. It will be the economic equivalent of Winston Churchill's famous assessment of Neville Chamberlain: "You were given the choice between war and dishonor. You chose dishonor and you will have war."[43]

4

CONFEDERACY OF
DUNCES

We've got to stop being the stupid party.
—Louisiana governor Bobby Jindal, 2013[1]

Science was a Democrat thing.
—Landon "Tucker" Davis, an Interior
Department official, according to notes by the
Interior Department's Office of Inspector General[2]

As with most if not all large, successful political parties and movements, a body of intellectual work makes the case for a center-right party in America. The essential texts would include F. A. Hayek's *Road to Serfdom*, Russell Kirk's *Conservative Mind*, Edmund Burke's *Reflections on the Revolution in France*, and Richard Weaver's *Ideas Have Consequences*. These are serious works by serious minds who have dedicated much of their intellectual life to examining the relationship between individuals and government, the true meaning of freedom, and what system of government affords individuals the greatest opportunity to maximize their potential.

The American conservative movement evolved after World

War II in different and often contradictory directions. In *The Conservative Intellectual Movement in America,* George Nash has a chapter titled "What Is Conservatism in America? The Search for a Viable Heritage." In it he quoted from William Schlamm, who is seen as the "father" of the *National Review* in that he encouraged William Buckley to found the magazine. The Austrian-born Schlamm, who had been such a fervent Communist that he had actually met Vladimir Lenin, made the case that there was no conservative historical tradition in America and for a reason:

> The American *species* (to the extent that there really is such a thing) is, of course, populist rather than conservative—and for a very forceful reason: America happens to be the only society in creation built by *conscious* human intent . . . and developed, by Europeans *tired* of Europe's ancient commitments, and determined, . . . each in his own way, on a "new beginning."[3]

Schlamm saw this as an opportunity to craft a new brand of American conservatism that must succeed not because of a historical tradition but because of "its moral and aesthetic superiority." This is the role he thought a new conservative magazine like the *National Review* could play. Today in the Trump era, many conservatives who believe Trump has denigrated all political discourse and destroyed any meaning of conservatism—which, of course, he has—look back longingly at the *National Review* as being everything that Trump World is not: clever, erudite, committed to principle. But what is often forgotten is that the *National Review* began as basically a well-educated-racist publication. In an infamous editorial published in 1957, Buckley fiercely defended segregation:

> The central question that emerges . . . is whether the White community in the South is entitled to take such measures as are necessary to prevail, politically and culturally, in areas in which it does not predominate numerically? The sobering answer is Yes—the White community is so entitled because, for the time being, it is the advanced race. It is not easy, and it is unpleasant, to adduce statistics evidencing the cultural superiority of White over Negro: but it is a fact that obtrudes, one that cannot be hidden by ever-so-busy egalitarians and anthropologists. . . .
>
> *National Review* believes that the South's premises are correct. . . . It is more important for any community, anywhere in the world, to affirm and live by civilized standards, than to bow to the demands of the numerical majority. Sometimes it becomes impossible to assert the will of a minority, in which case it must give way; and the society will regress; sometimes the numerical minority cannot prevail except by violence: then it must determine whether the prevalence of its will is worth the terrible price of violence.[4]

Buckley loved to be a provocateur—when he ran for mayor of New York and was asked what he would do if he won, his response was, "Demand a recount"—but his defense of segregation wasn't a Swiftian piece of fancy meant to stir up a debate.[5] The *National Review,* as the unofficial intellectual beating heart of the American conservative movement, was committed to the principle that a "white" culture was superior to all others. William Schlamm went on to edit the John Birch Society magazine, *American Opinion.* In 1965 at the Cambridge Union, Buckley debated James Baldwin on the topic "The American Dream Is at the Expense of the American Negro."

It was an extraordinary exchange and one of the few moments when Buckley faced an opponent more eloquent in word and elegant and appearance. James Baldwin slaughtered William Buckley; at the conclusion of the debate, 544 supported the Baldwin argument and 164 the Buckley side. The losing Buckley argument was one that would continue to be a touchstone of the Republican credo on race until today: that in America, race doesn't matter; anyone can succeed. It is the essence of the "color blind" assertion that is perversely racist but reassuring to white people. It has the benefits of sounding antiracist—we are all people, or, as it were, "all lives matter"—but is in practice deeply racist because it ignores the reality of the impact of race in every element of American society. James Baldwin took his audience through a journey of what it meant to be black in America:

> It comes as a great shock around the age of 5, 6 or 7 to discover that the flag to which you have pledged allegiance, along with everybody else, has not pledged allegiance to you. . . . I picked cotton, I carried it to the

market, I built the railroads under someone else's whip
for nothing. . . . The American soil is full of the corpses
of my ancestors. . . . Why is my freedom, my citizenship,
in question now?

Buckley's response was to deny the existence of race as a
societal force:

It is quite impossible in my judgment to deal with the
indictments of Mr. Baldwin unless one is prepared to
deal with him as a white man, unless one is prepared to
say to him that the fact that your skin is black is utterly
irrelevant to the arguments you raise.

He then pivoted to the argument that is also used today
by Republicans, that being black in America is actually an
advantage because government and society treat blacks with a
differential preference:

Mr. Baldwin, I am going to speak to you without any
reference whatever to those surrounding protections
which you are used to in virtue of the fact that you are a
Negro. . . . My great-grandparents were presumably your
worth also.[6]

Many current anti-Trump Republicans wax nostalgic about
the days of the intellectual firepower of the *National Review,*
but the truth is that Trump's racism is a direct descendant of
William Buckley's early racism. By 2004, Buckley would say,

"I once believed we could evolve our way up from Jim Crow. I was wrong. Federal intervention was necessary."[7] Instead of obsessing over language to communicate with African American voters and those of lower income, Republicans should face the reality that many in these demographics view government as a positive and necessary tool in bettering their lives. The avowed hatred of government that is such a Republican bedrock principle is offensive and alienating to much of the country. A constant crowd-pleasing refrain of Ronald Reagan's sums it up: "The nine most terrifying words in the English language are 'I'm from the government, and I'm here to help.' "[8] For most white Americans of the middle class, that strikes them as both funny and poignant. (It is also a practice of the white middle class to be completely blind to the vast help they get from the government in all aspects of their lives.) But how does a black person hear these same words, knowing that it took thirty thousand federal troops to force the University of Mississippi to accept one African American?[9]

When George W. Bush ran for president in 2000, he made a conscious effort to make the case for a conservative role of government that could also be compassionate, hence the phrase "compassionate conservatism." I moved to Austin, Texas, in the spring of 1999 and later wrote a book about the campaign, *The Big Enchilada*.[10] The entire conceit of compassionate conservatism was an acknowledgment that conservatism had failed to provide an alternative to the conservative critique that liberals believed any problem could be solved through more money and more government. As Steve Goldsmith, then mayor of Indianapolis and the chief domestic policy adviser for Bush, put it, "The Republicans' message was that government had been harmful. Therefore, eliminate government, and people in tough circumstances will suddenly be better off. Both the public and many Republican mayors said that's naive. Merely the absence of bad action is not going to be sufficient."[11]

When I first joined the Bush campaign, Karl Rove handed me a copy of *The Dream and the Nightmare: The Sixties' Legacy to the Underclass* by Myron Magnet. "Read it," Karl said. "This is what the governor wants to talk about." I'd never heard of Magnet and promptly devoured the book. It was an elegant description of a conservative alternative to deeply rooted problems of contemporary American society, from government's role in enabling generations of welfare dependency to the success of Mayor Rudy Giuliani's approach to law enforcement that had greatly reduced crime in New York City. It fell to the speechwriter Michael Gerson to put many of the themes addressed by Magnet into words that would be emotionally powerful and politically persuasive. Phrases like "the soft bigotry of low expectations" to describe a failed education system that processed children more than educated them, or "reading is the first civil right," or celebrating those involved in private efforts to help those in need as "the armies of compassion."

A year or so into the Trump presidency, it occurred to me that so many of the most strident voices against Trump were those I'd worked with in the Bush campaigns: Michael Gerson, now a *Washington Post* columnist; Nicolle Wallace, who has her own show on MSNBC; Steve Schmidt, who ran rapid response for the 2004 Bush campaign; Matthew Dowd, who coordinated polling in the 2000 campaign and was a 2004 strategist turned ABC regular; and Mark McKinnon, who, along with Karl Rove, brought me into the Bush world and now has a show, *The Circus,* on Showtime. Years ago we often worked together in the same room, and individually we have reacted to Donald Trump with like disgust and dismay. Excepting a few times on Nicolle's show, I've actually never spoken with any of my former campaign workers about Trump, but it's easy to understand why we are all saying the same thing in different ways. The embrace of Trump by the Republican Party is a repudiation of everything we claimed to believe. We felt that we were part of a movement to prove that a "different kind of Republican," as we sometimes described Bush (intentionally ripping off Clinton's "different kind of Democrat" 1992 slogan), could redefine conservatism. There was a basic humanity and decency about George W. Bush that we believed could draw those who had been alienated by the harshness of conservatism into giving Bush a second look.

Today it's impossible to imagine a candidate running on George W. Bush's definition of conservatism having any chance of success in a Republican primary. Jeb Bush lost for many reasons, but the basic one is that he was running to win a race in a party that no longer existed. He was like a guy who showed up with a tennis racket at a bowling alley. But in retrospect, I have to wonder if the party that many of us thought was defined by George W. Bush ever really existed, at least in the incarnation we believed. A year or so into the Trump presidency, I reread *The Dream and the Nightmare,* assuming it would remind me of what it was we aspired to and refresh a sense of hope of what could emerge after Trump. Instead, it filled me with dread, starting with the preface that Magnet wrote for a new edition issued in 2000:

The Dream and the Nightmare was the first book to argue that culture, not racism or lack of jobs or the welfare system, was the cause of the underclass. I didn't mean that the culprit was some "culture of poverty" or "ghetto culture." The problem, I contended, lay in the majority culture. Led by its elite institutions—the universities, the judiciary, the press, the great charitable foundations, even the mainstream churches—American culture underwent a revolution in the 1960s, which transformed some of its most basic beliefs and values, including its beliefs about the causes of poverty. When these new attitudes reached the poor, and particularly the urban, minority poor, the result was catastrophic: Many of the new culture's beliefs downplayed the personal responsibility, self-control, and deferral of gratification that it takes to succeed. At the same time, the new culture celebrated an "if it feels good, do it" self-indulgence that for the poor, whose lives have less margin for error than the prosperous, too often proved disastrous. The social policy that these ideas engendered compounded the disaster.

In Magnet's view, the 1960s were a time when America lost its way and became disconnected from the moorings of culture and faith that had . . . made America great. What I realized I was reading was an articulate, erudite evocation of the world as seen by Donald Trump. The period of some of the most dramatic and uplifting social change in America, a time when millions of Americans were granted the right to vote after pitched battles were fought in the streets, that was not the civil rights era we should celebrate but the time in which America lost its way. White families own more than 90 percent of the wealth in America not because of institutionalized racism and the legacy of slavery but rather because of their "culture." In Magnet's world,

> economic opportunity is meaningful only if individuals are culturally equipped to seize it. Cultural values such as neatness, punctuality, thoroughness, and dependability are the causes, not the results, of economic mobility. The same is even more true of such cultural traits as ambition, entrepreneurialism, respect for education, or pushing one's children to succeed.

Magnet is neither a racist nor an ignorant man. In a chapter titled "Race and Reparations," he acknowledged,

> Two centuries of slavery and another of discrimination and segregation did indeed produce victims on a world-historical scale. Today's black poverty is the most visible reminder of a history filled with equal measures of pain and shame on the subject of race.

But this fine and elegant mind looked around America in 1993 and concluded that the success of some blacks must prove that the institutional barriers to success for all blacks have been removed:

> All this has meant that for years blacks have not been barred from the economic mainstream. What other conclusion can be drawn from the proliferation of the black middle class in the last quarter century? Though doors still remain to be unlocked, as a general principle opportunity is open for whoever wishes to seek it.[12]

When I read this in 1999, did I really believe it? Twenty years later, after eight years of an African American president and the longest bull market in U.S. history, the disparity between white and black economic realities is staggering:

- Black workers earn over $11,000 less annually than white workers.
- Twenty percent of black and Hispanic Americans live in poverty, compared with less than 9 percent for whites.
- The median wealth for white Americans is $171,000, compared with $17,600 for black Americans.
- Less than half of black households are homeowners, compared with nearly three-quarters of white households.[13]

The comparisons stretch out in a depressingly long line. What is so unintentionally dangerous about the propositions asserted by Magnet and so many others like him is that they give an intellectual justification for an entire industry of hate that has come to dominate the Republican Party. Not many Americans know Myron Magnet or his work, but they know Rush Limbaugh, Sean Hannity, Alex Jones, Lou Dobbs, and an endless stream of professional nuts and cranks who roam the internet selling conspiracies, bitterness, grievance, and anger, in search of an argument. When Donald Trump tweets out a defense of "conservative thinkers like James Woods banned from Twitter, and Paul Watson banned from Facebook," the immediate instinct is to burst out laughing at the image of a cranky old actor and a maladjusted British weirdo whose mentor is Alex Jones elevated to some intellectual standing.[14] But actually Trump is dead right: Woods and Watson are the conservative thinkers of the day.

Once you convince yourself that racism has been defeated and that the real problems in America are the crisis of the family structure, it's a short walk to the impeached Alabama judge and defeated Senate candidate Roy Moore's passionate claim that blacks were better off during slavery. America was great, Moore claimed, because "families were united—even though we had slavery. They cared for one another. People were strong in the families."[15]

Today the intellectual leaders of the Republican Party are the paranoids, kooks, know-nothings, and bigots who once could be heard only on late-night talk shows, the stations you listened to on long drives because it was hard to fall asleep while laughing. When any political movement loses all sense of self and has no unifying theory of government, it ceases to function as a collective rooted in thought and becomes more like fans of a sports team. Asking the Republican Party today to agree on a definition of conservatism is like asking New York Giants fans to have a consensus opinion on the Law of the Sea Treaty. It's not just that no one knows anything about the subject; they don't remotely care. All Republicans want to do is beat the team playing the Giants. They aren't voters using active intelligence or participants in a civil democracy; they are fans. Their role is to cheer and fund their team and trash-talk whatever team is on the other side. This removes any of the seeming contradiction of having spent years supporting principles like free trade and personal responsibility to suddenly stop and support the opposite. Think of those principles like players on a team. You cheered for them when they were on your team, but then management fired them or traded them to another team, so of course you aren't for them anymore. If your team suddenly decides to focus on running instead of passing, no fan cares—as long as the team wins.

Stripped of any pretense of governing philosophy, a political party will default to being controlled by those who shout the loudest and are unhindered by any semblance of normalcy. It isn't the quiet fans in the stands who get on television but the lunatics who paint their bodies with the team colors and go shirtless on frigid days. It's the crazy person who lunges at the ref and jumps over seats to fight the other team's fans who is cheered by his fellow fans as he is led away on the jumbotron. What is the forum in which the key issues of the day are discussed? Talk radio and the television shows sponsored by the team, like *Fox & Friends,* Tucker Carlson, and Sean Hannity.

One of the hallmarks of the Trump era is the alacrity with

which intelligent people embrace stupidity. As it was in Mao's China with the Red Guard, it is a political crime in today's Republican Party to appear well educated. So we find Senator Josh Hawley of Missouri tweeting a rant about "unelected progressive elites in our govt."[16] The senator went to Stanford, taught at St. Paul's School in London (founded in 1509), and graduated from Yale Law School. Senator Ted Cruz denounces "coastal elites who attack the NRA."[17] Cruz was born in Calgary, Canada, graduated from Princeton and Harvard Law School, was a Supreme Court clerk, worked in the Bush administration, and is a former assistant attorney general. His wife was born in the coastal town of San Luis Obispo, California, and holds a BA from Claremont McKenna College, an MA from Université Libre de Bruxelles, and an MBA from Harvard Business School. She works as a managing director at Goldman Sachs. Heidi Cruz came to national attention when Donald Trump tweeted out an unflattering picture of her next to his wife, Melania, during the Republican primary in 2016 with the line "A picture says a thousand words."[18] His wife, Melania, is a former nude model with a high school degree.

The Harvard Law graduate and former secretary of education William Bennett wrote a best-selling book, *The Death of Outrage: Bill Clinton and the Assault on American Ideals,* in which he assailed President Clinton for his deeply flawed character.[19] "A president whose character manifests itself in patterns of reckless personal conduct, deceit, abuse of power, and contempt for the rule of law cannot be a good president," he wrote.[20] His most popular book was titled *The Book of Virtues.* No one on the right had argued more strenuously for the importance of character:

People of good character are not all going to come down on the same side of difficult political and social issues. Good people—people of character and moral literacy— can be conservative, and good people can be liberal. We must not permit our disputes over thorny political questions to obscure the obligation we have to offer instruction to all our young people in the area in which we have, as a society, reached a consensus: namely, on the importance of good character, and some of its pervasive particulars.[21]

But when Trump emerged from the primary, Bennett characterized those Republicans not supporting Trump as not team players who "suffer from a terrible case of moral superiority and put their own vanity and taste above the interest of the country."[22]

What has changed? If he believed what he wrote in *The Book of Virtues* that "it is our character that supports the promise of our future—far more than particular government programs or policies," if he believed what he wrote about Bill Clinton that "a president whose character manifests itself in patterns of reckless personal conduct . . . cannot be a good president," how can Bennett support a man who brags about assaulting women and directs his own son to write checks to reimburse his lawyer Michael Cohen for hush payments to a porn star?[23]

When Bill Bennett wrote *The Book of Virtues* and *The Death of Outrage,* he was serving a role needed in all civil societies: intellectual leaders in the public square speak out when they feel a society is adrift from its basic principles. That many disagreed with him is a healthy sign of a self-questioning society, and indeed that very debate is as important as any of the specifics raised. Not to question is to accept and condone. The essence of Bennett's arguments for the role of character in a society was a plea based on decency and patriotism, not partisanship.

So what sort of signal does it send when a man as intelligent and thoughtful as Bill Bennett decides to contradict his entire body of work to support a man like Donald Trump? What value is left in intelligent reasoning? Donald Trump didn't crash the guardrails of political and civil standards; rather, the highway officials eagerly removed the guardrails and stood by cheering as the lunatic behind the wheel drove the party straight off the cliff of reason. When a Williams College and Harvard Law grad like Bill Bennett considers a man who found the nuclear triad a puzzling mystery in a primary debate qualified to be president, the idiotocracy is in full ascendant.

John F. Kennedy once held a dinner for all the living Nobel Prize laureates at the White House. Donald Trump invited the CEO of Twitter, Jack Dorsey, to the White House so that he could complain about his Twitter account. Trump holds to a theory that there is some vast left-wing conspiracy in the tech world illuminati to personally slight him at every opportunity. But that's just one of the many conspiracies that Trump embraces. There is a "Deep State" cabal out to get him. The Deep State seems to be driven by Trump's annoyance that there was a government that existed before he came to power and there is a government that will exist afterward. (The latter may be overly optimistic.) He lost the popular vote due to massive voter fraud. He agreed with Infowars' Alex Jones that Hillary Clinton might have taken some form of drugs to enhance her debate performance and demanded, "I think we should take a drug test prior to the debate. I do."[24] Trump attacked his primary opponent Senator Ted Cruz by linking his father to the JFK assassination. He has said that a pillow was found on the Supreme Court justice Antonin Scalia's face and he might have been murdered. He's sided with the anti-vaccine conspiracy nuts. Most famously, he laid the groundwork for his campaign for the Republican nomination by promising he could prove President Barack Obama was born in Africa. He's claimed President Obama wore a ring with an Arabic inscription. He's said global warming is a "hoax," that windmills cause cancer.

In their analysis of the rise of conspiracies in conservative politics, *A Lot of People Are Saying*, Russell Muirhead and Nancy Rosenblum describe the connection between Republicans and the need for conspiracies:

> The new conspiracism has what we call a "partisan penumbra," an alignment with radical, antigovernment Republicans. Not all Republicans or conservatives join these ranks, but . . . they rarely speak out against conspiracist claims. They exhibit partisan reticence. And while the Left participates in its share of classic conspiracy theories, it has not yet taken up the new conspiracism. What we have, then, is an alignment between the extremes of the Republican Party and the

new conspiracism—a congruence founded in hostility toward government. These conspiracist claims persist in the United States even when Republicans themselves control government. Today, conspiracism is not, as we might expect, the last resort of permanent political losers but the first resort of winners. Trump refuses to accept the terms of his own victory and incessantly conjures machinations against him, including coups d'état from within his own administration.

But partisan politics is far from the whole story. For what unites conspiracists is not ideological attachment to conservative causes or to the Republican Party but something deeper: disdain for political opposition, regulated party rivalry, and the democratic norm of "agreeing to disagree." Each conspiracist assault is specific to one candidate or policy or party, but it eventually extends to them all. It is not contained.[25]

Donald Trump's mind is that tabloid you see at the checkout counter of the grocery store claiming that aliens impregnated Chelsea Clinton so the offspring could become president and turn the United States over to the Federation. Few Republicans challenge Trump on his conspiracy obsessions, treating him like an addled senior citizen who calls his congressman's office demanding to know why the CIA is talking to him through his dentures. The shrug and smile that so many Republican leaders have adopted has allowed Trump to dismiss those who challenge his lunacy as "angry Democrats," because it is Democrats who seem capable of explaining that Ted Cruz's dad didn't kill JFK. But Trump isn't an addled senior citizen—

actually he is, but he's one who happens to be the president of the United States. The acceptance of the conspiracy theories is just one station in the slaughterhouse of truth that is the Trump presidency. Once there is no challenge to the craziest of ideas that have no basis in fact, it is easy for Trump to take one small bit of truth and spin it into an elaborate fantasy.

This is how Trump can turn a thousand or so South Americans seeking asylum into "an invasion" that threatens the security of the country. A meeting with Kim Jong Un becomes a declaration that "there is no longer a Nuclear Threat from North Korea."[26] "Puerto Rico got 91 Billion Dollars for the hurricane. . . . The pols are grossly incompetent, spend the money foolishly or corruptly, & only take from USA," he tweets.[27] In truth, Puerto Rico is part of the United States and has received less than $14 billion. Facebook bans dangerous conspiracy nuts like Alex Jones and his English protégé Paul Joseph Watson, and Trump defends them, calling the ban an attack on "conservatives." His followers promptly call for government control of tech industries.

Republicans are allowing Trump to equate conservatism with conspiracy, and the long-term success is predicated on stupidity becoming an airborne viral plague that will sweep the country like the walking dead. That seems like a bad bet for a political party, but one on which the truth-shredding, anti-fact Republicans are betting the future of a sane, respected center-right political party in America. Trump has staged a national Scopes Trial and placed himself in the William Jennings Bryan role. The question for the Republican Party is whether it is content to let the Democratic Party play Clarence Darrow. All indications are overwhelmingly yes.

5

MACHINERY OF DECEPTION

> He is free to evade reality, he is free to unfocus his
> mind and stumble blindly down any road he pleases,
> but not free to avoid the abyss he refuses to see.
>
> —Ayn Rand[1]

Years ago, my firm was working on a supreme court race in Alabama for a client running against Roy Moore in the Republican primary. At the time we used a female actress for voice-over work on a lot of commercials. When she read the script we had written for our client, she balked at recording it because of its conservative message. "Jennifer," my partner explained, "what you have to understand is that we're working for the liberal in the race." (Her name wasn't Jennifer, but she later became a Tony Award–winning star, and I wouldn't want to embarrass her about past day job work.) She laughed, but it was true. Our guy was a real Alabama conservative, but he did have respect for the rule of law, and he would never have been removed from office, as was Moore. Actually, Moore was removed from the Alabama Supreme Court, in 2003 and 2017. The first removal came after he constructed a giant memorial to the Ten Commandments inside the Alabama Supreme

Court building and refused to remove it under court order. Earlier, as a circuit judge, Moore had hung a plaque with the Ten Commandments in his courtroom, and his fight to keep the Ten Commandments displayed had helped boost him to chief justice of the state supreme court. Figuring it was good for his box office, Moore doubled down once he was chief justice and replaced the plaque with a full-on, mausoleum-worthy hunk of granite.[2]

The fight over the Ten Commandments monument got Moore national news, and he became something of a cult figure for many in Alabama. But what few knew was that a video of the monument was made and sold by a company that helped Moore pay for his legal expenses over the fight that led to his removal from the supreme court.[3] That little detail perfectly encapsulates the monetization of phony morality that is so common with the professional Christian conservatives. Six days after being removed from office for the second time, Moore announced his candidacy for the Republican nomination for senator in a special election to fill the seat vacated by Donald Trump's appointment of Jeff Sessions as attorney general. Despite multiple allegations of molesting an underage girl, sexual harassment of barely legal teenage girls, and being such a general creep that he was allegedly banned from his local mall in Gadsden, Alabama, Moore defeated the appointed incumbent Luther Strange and became the Republican nominee.

When Moore won the nomination, Donald Trump and the Republican National Committee endorsed him. Trump supported Moore's denials, and on Election Day Moore won

67 percent of white voters.[4] Only black voters, particularly black women who turned out at record levels, saved the state of Alabama from being represented by an accused child molester who said that he first noticed his wife when he saw her in a high school dance performance. Moore was thirty at the time.[5] What sort of man goes to high school dance performances to check out the girls? The Roy Moore race was a perfect test to see if there really was any decency left in the national Republican Party, and the answer came back clearly: not very much. The Alabama Senate race was somewhere between a bad bar joke and a perfect political science experiment: "What would it take to get white Republicans in Alabama to support a Democrat? What if the Republican was a child molester?" By Election Day, nine women had come forward with allegations against Moore. No credible defense was offered by Moore or his supporters other than a blanket denial. As Donald Trump said, "He denies it."[6] Just as Trump himself had denied sexual harassment accusations of the many women who came forward during his campaign. Does this mean Alabama is pro–child molesting of underage girls? Does Trump's winning mean that America is pro–sexual harassment? There's certainly an element of lack of concern about women and the sense that women are fair game for men, even fifteen-year-old girls. But mostly it shows an ability of many conservative voters to live in a self-reinforcing bubble that has little to do with objective truth. From denials of child molesting and sexual harassment to the overwhelming science of global warming, an element of American conservatism has grown over decades in an environment distinct from the

rest of the country (and reality), nurtured by an ever-growing ecosphere of alternative truth.

The dystopian Shangri-La that so many on the right inhabit was years in the making. If it often seems that the Republican Party is living in a world disconnected from reality, that's because it is. Large elements of the Republican Party have made a collective decision that there is no objective truth. *Network Propaganda: Manipulation, Disinformation, and Radicalization in American Politics,* published in 2018, is the most extensive comparison of the Democratic and Republican Parties' relationship to the media and a concept of verifiable truth. Its analysis highlighted the differences between the two parties:

> We did not come to this work looking for a partisan-skewed explanation. As we began to analyze the millions of online stories, tweets, and Facebook sharing data points, the pattern that emerged was clear. Our own earlier work, which analyzed specific campaigns around intellectual property law and found that right and left online media collaborated, made us skeptical of our initial observations, but these proved highly resilient to a wide range of specifications and robustness checks. Something very different was happening in right-wing media than in centrist, center-left, and left-wing media. We will make the argument throughout this book that the behavior of the right-wing media ecosystem repre-sents a radicalization of roughly a third of the American media system. We use the term "radicalization" advis-

edly in two senses. First, to speak of "polarization" is to assume symmetry. No fact emerges more clearly from our analysis of how four million political stories were linked, tweeted, and shared over a three-year period than that there is no symmetry in the architecture and dynamics of communications within the right-wing media ecosystem and outside of it.[7]

In this restrained and scholarly presentation is a screaming headline that, yes, Republicans have gone crazy and here's proof. The authors—Yochai Benkler, Robert Faris, and Hal Roberts—remind readers of the critical role played by modern institutions that serve as gatekeepers for an accepted truth. Since the end of World War II, this trend toward institutionalized professions for truth seeking has accelerated. Government statistics agencies, scientific and academic investigations, law and the legal profession, and journalism developed increasingly rationalized and formalized solutions to the problem of how societies made up of diverse populations with diverse and conflicting political views can nonetheless form a shared sense of what is going on in the world. As the quip usually attributed to Daniel Patrick Moynihan put it, "Everyone is entitled to his own opinion, but not his own facts."[8] Politics was always centrally about identity and belonging and meaning, but in the decades following World War II, democracy operated within constraints with regard to a shared set of institutional statements about reality.

It's instructive that the writers use "reality" as a synonym for the "truth" because at its heart that's really what is at stake: Does a society live in a shared reality? In a civil society like the United States, that shared reality, that truth, is the core energy that drives the functioning of society. Without agreement that red lights tell motorists to stop, there is no traffic control. (Try driving in Brazil or the Central African Republic to test that theory.) It doesn't work if some drivers think red means you must stop, some think it means you can stop, and others think it means to speed up. The same applies to countless threads that weave together to create a coherent society. I've spent much of the last thirty years—far too much, in retrospect—arguing with the press about various lies, half-truths, and deceptions foisted upon the voting public by Democratic candidates and their party operatives. More than most, I can bear testimony to the regular use of deceit to push Democratic campaigns. The fact-checking website PolitiFact gave President Obama its 2013 "Lie of the Year" award for his repeated assurance that under Obamacare "if you like your health care plan, you can keep it."[9] A couple of years earlier, it gave the Democratic Party the same award for the coordinated Democratic message that Republicans were plotting to "end Medicare."[10]

But if I'm going to be honest about honesty, I have to admit that I saw in practice—okay, I participated in—the process the authors of *Network Propaganda* found through their research. Republicans have built a political ecosphere that thrives on deceit and lies. It is an industrialized sort of deceit that is unique to the Republican Party. Over the last decades, Republicans have been conducting an experiment to determine how many control rods of truth could be taken

out of a civil society's core reactor of truth without creating
a meltdown. It didn't start with Trump, but Trump may prove
to be the meltdown.

What few people grasp—because they are outside the
system and have normal lives to lead—is just how huge the
machinery of deception is that the Republicans have erected
and how long it has been in the making. Fox News is unique
in American media history as serving more like the in-house
propaganda arm of a strong-man dictator than operating by
the accepted norms of professional journalism. But Fox News
did not spring fancifully into being as the creation of a former
political consultant named Roger Ailes with the help of an
immigrant who failed to assimilate American values, Rupert
Murdoch. For decades a certain percentage of those who
called themselves conservatives had been cultivating a country
within a country, a sort of virtual secession from the United
States of America. Like Donald Trump's election, Fox News
was both an inevitable conclusion and an accelerant. Nicole
Hemmer, a professor at the University of Virginia's Miller
Center, became intrigued by her father's devotion to conservative talk radio and television and embarked on a study of the
history of the conservative media world. The result, *Messengers of the Right: Conservative Media and the Transformation
of American Politics,* published in 2016, surprised her:

> I uncovered a network of activism far broader and far
> more influential than I had expected. Beginning in the
> late 1940s and 1950s, activists working in media emerged
> as leaders of the conservative movement. Not only did

they start an array of media enterprises—publishing houses, radio programs, magazines, book clubs, television shows—they built the movement. They coordinated rallies, founded organizations, ran political campaigns, and mobilized voters. From the archives they emerged as a distinct group that I call "media activists," men and women (but mostly men) whose primary sites of activism were the media institutions they founded. While they disagreed profoundly on tactics and strategy, they shared a belief that political change stemmed not just from ideas but from the proper expression and diffusion of those ideas through ideological media sources. Unlike fellow conservatives who worked for mainstream periodicals and broadcasters, these media activists believed independence was vital to their work—that they needed to develop their own publishing houses, their own radio programs, their own magazines if they were going to truly change American politics.[11]

These days the branding of Fox News as "Fair and Balanced" often seems primarily to serve the purpose of proving that irony is not dead. But there is a long history within the far right of right-wing media positioning itself as the only true and honest media. To promote a world viewpoint distinct from that shared by the majority, it was critical to assert that everyone else simply didn't have the correct information on which to base decisions. That is a far easier task than accusing most of the country of being crazy. So in the 1950s, if your neighbor didn't believe that Communists had infiltrated the local school board, it was just because he or she didn't know how to spot a Communist. As Hemmer wrote in a piece for *The Atlantic:*

> The idea of "fair and balanced" partisan media has its roots in the 1940s and 1950s. *Human Events,* the right-wing newsweekly founded in 1944, was dedicated to publishing the "facts" other outlets overlooked. Yet while touting this fact-based approach, the editors were also dedicated to promoting a distinct point of view. By the early 1960s, *Human Events* arrived at this formulation of its mission:
>
> "In reporting the news, *Human Events* is objective; it aims for accurate representation of the facts. But it is not impartial. It looks at events through eyes that are biased in favor of limited constitutional government, local self-government, private enterprise, and individual freedom."
>
> In distinguishing between objectivity and impartiality, *Human Events'* editors created a space where "bias" was an appropriate journalistic value, one that could work in tandem with objectivity.[12]

The entire ecosphere of right-wing media that exists today can be traced back to the four-page pamphlet that two journalists started in 1944 and called *Human Events.* Given the current unequivocal embrace within conservative media of all things military and the reliable support for any American military action, it is extraordinary to consider that the two founders were committed pacifists who had belonged to the America First movement prior to World War II and continued to oppose the war even after Pearl Harbor. There was a toxic strain of anti-Semitism in the America First movement quite content to see Hitler deal with Europe's "Jewish problem." But the co-founders of *Human Events*, Felix Morley and Frank Hanighen, both came out of Haverford College, the Pennsylvania college founded by Quakers, and viewed with great suspicion what Dwight Eisenhower would later refer to as the "military-industrial complex." In 1934, Hanighen had co-authored an exposé of the international arms business titled "The Merchants of Death."[13] In 1942, Morley had written a piece for *The Saturday Evening Post*, "For What Are We Fighting?" that did the almost unimaginable by challenging the need to fight a war America had entered after Pearl Harbor.[14] But the criticism they received only further convinced Morley and Hanighen that they saw the world clearly, resisting the siren call of patriotism without thought. They saw themselves as keepers of a true journalistic flame of honesty, opposing the corrupting alliance of government and media that had united to promote a war they thought was immoral. After the first year, Morley wrote, "This little publication represents the protest of two experienced American journalists against the loss of standards in contemporary American writing on current events. These standards have been a wartime casualty."[15] In that positioning was the framing of the relationship between their audience and what would later be called the "mainstream media" that continues to this day. Their attitude was clear: we see the world as it really is, uncorrupted by the powerful forces that manipulate the rest of the press and much of the public. As Nicole Hemmer wrote in *Messengers of the Right,*

> They believed mainstream American journalists were shutting out alternative points of view, that they were "coloring, slanting, selecting and editing the news" in order to tamp down any criticisms of the war. Morley argued that in trumpeting the official line doled out by government agencies, journalists had played a role in the "subtle regimentation of public opinion." Never one to shy away from a Nazi comparison, he added, "While we have not yet carried these practices as far as did the unlamented Dr. Goebbels, the general direction of governmental propaganda has paid that Nazi leader the sincerest form of flattery."[16]

The small D.C. apartment where Morley and Hanighen started *Human Events* is, to the industries of right-wing media that follow, what Steve Jobs's garage was to the tech world. An heir to a Chicago-based textile fortune, Henry Regnery stepped in to help fund and promote what was basically no more than a newsletter. Regnery used *Human Events* as the first effort to launch Regnery Publishing, which would become the dominant publisher for conservative books and still thrives today. Astonishingly, considering its later course, one of the first publications of Regnery's new publishing venture was *Blueprint for World Conquest,* a collection of documents from the Communist International. This was followed by several books that were, as Hemmer wrote, "revisionist works on Germany: Victor Gollancz's *Our Threatened Values* (1946) and *In Darkest Germany* (1947), and a translation of Max Picard's *Hitler in Our Selves* (1947). The books, which were critical of the Allied treatment of Germany and the postwar order, did not sell, but Regnery didn't mind."[17]

In 1951, Regnery agreed to publish William Buckley's *God and Man at Yale,* the book that secured the role of both Regnery's publishing house and Bill Buckley in the coming conservative wars. Eager to have the book available for the 250th anniversary of Yale, Buckley got his father to kick in $3,000 to cover costs for expedited publication, then another $17,000 for publicity, making the conservative classic close to a self-published book. *God and Man at Yale* became a *New York Times* best seller, and Buckley followed it up with a defense of Joseph McCarthy written with his brother-in-law Brent Bozell, *McCarthy and His Enemies: The Record and Its Meaning.*[18] Like his defense of segregation in the *National Review,* the McCarthy book is a reminder for those who today, in the age of Trump, like to cast William Buckley as the lost soul of true conservatism: that for all his well-crafted sentences and love of language, Buckley was often a more articulate version of the same deep ugliness and bigotry that is the hallmark of Trumpism. If nothing else, *McCarthy and His Enemies* prompted one of the classic negative reviews of literary history, a brief treatment by Philip Kurland, a University of Chicago Law School professor, that reflects the disdain of Buckley by the liberal academic establishment he loved to attack:

This volume is the development of a theme expressed by Christopher Fry's mayor in *The Lady's Not for Burning:*

"That's enough!
Terrible frivolity, terrible blasphemy,
Awful unorthodoxy. I can't understand
Anything that's being said. Fetch a constable.
The woman's tongue clearly knows the flavour
Of *spiritu maligno*. The man must be
Drummed out of this town."

Buckley wrote another book which Regnery published. This is more of the same.[19]

After investing in Regnery Publishing, William Buckley's father helped launch the *Manion Forum of Opinion,* a weekly radio show hosted by Clarence Manion, a former dean at the Notre Dame Law School. Like the founders of *Human Events,* Clarence "Pat" Manion had taken an unlikely path to becoming one of the brightest stars in the conservative galaxy. He came from an upper-middle-class family in northern Kentucky and studied philosophy at Catholic University in Washington. Rick Perlstein in *Before the Storm* paints the scene of what it was like for a young, idealistic Democrat like Manion who was strongly opposed to America's involvement in a war in Europe:

Woodrow Wilson had captured Washington from the stolid, stand-pat Republicans. The nation's capital was teeming with brash young intellectuals from all over the country who believed the progressive mood percolating through the states had finally found its fit exemplar in the former political science professor now in the White House. He had resisted the entreaties of Wall Street and had pledged that under his Administration no American would suffer entanglement in the blood feud then raging in Europe. Manion, too young to vote, was swept up in the excitement. The night before the 1916 election he stood in front of Democratic headquarters and led the chants for reelection: "We want peace, we don't want war. / We want Wilson four years more!"[20]

Manion was disillusioned but remained a Democrat and went on to write a textbook that explained it was a government's duty to guarantee all citizens a certain standard of living. His continuing isolationist and antiwar attitude pushed him into becoming rabidly anti-Roosevelt. He left Notre Dame in 1952 and supported Robert Taft based on his foreign policy. Perlstein describes how Manion

> became one of the nation's foremost advocates for the strange foreign policy mishmash cooked up by Ohio senator Robert Taft, leader of the conservative forces in Congress: anticommunism for isolationists. Like their internationalist cousins, Taftites held that the Communist conspiracy was America's eternal enemy. But they also believed that America's antecedent eternal enemy—what George Washington warned of in his farewell address as "entangling alliances"—was worse. The solution to this contradiction was the belief that policies such as signing mutual security pacts in the NATO mold

and pledging foreign aid to vulnerable nations sapped America's ability to fight the menace at home, where the real threat was, from traitors like Alger Hiss and Owen Lattimore, and the agents in the federal government who would bring America to her knees through social spending that would cripple the economy through inflation—Russia's most devious offensive of all. (One theory had it that Harry Dexter White, the former Treasury Department official who went on to become director of the International Monetary Fund, stole U.S. Mint engraving plates so that Communism could flood the country with excess currency.)[21]

You can draw a straight line from that blend of kooky conspiracy theory, anti–foreign alliances, and instinctual victimhood to Donald Trump's worldview. In Trump's world, the internal forces conspiring against the country are the Deep State, not the Communists, but it is a vision of the world through a heavy fog of paranoia and fear. The steady conservatism of Eisenhower is unmasked not as governance that brought peace and prosperity to a postwar America but as a naive breeding ground that allows the rest of the world to take advantage of our too-generous benevolence. The *Manion Forum* radio program became a model for the talk radio empires of conservatives and a centerpiece in the movement that helped Barry Goldwater seize power in the Republican Party. In 1959, Manion helped organize the "Goldwater Committee of 100" that reached out on the radio and through direct mail, which was just beginning to take off as a conservative engine, to solicit contributions and build lists for the conservative movement. In 1960, William Buckley's brother-in-law and co-author of the book defending McCarthy, Brent Bozell, ghostwrote Goldwater's *Conscience of a Conservative,* which became to conservatives what Mao's *Little Red Book* was to the Red Guard. Others joined the *Manion Forum* radio show, as E. J. Dionne Jr. details in *Why the Right Went Wrong:*

> In the late 1950s, H. L. Hunt, the Texas oil millionaire, set up the Life Line Foundation, which included a news-letter, television programs, and a book club. Its greatest influence came in its radio program. By the end of 1962, as the scholar Mary Brennan noted, it was being broadcast 342 times a day on roughly 300 radio stations in 42 states and the District of Columbia. There was also Dan Smoot, a former FBI agent turned right-wing pamphle-teer and later a John Birch Society leader. He developed a substantial audience, with his radio program at one point reaching 150 stations and 16 million households weekly. Typical Smoot fare was his 1962 book, *The Invisible Government,* about the Council on Foreign Relations and its efforts to create "a one-world socialist system." It sold more than 2 million copies.[22]

But these conservative successes were dominated by journalism that operated under a shared code of standards and professionalism. The Federal Communications Commission's fairness doctrine was one limiting factor for conservatives, as described in *Network Propaganda:*

Most Americans got their news from the three broadcast networks. Radio still operated under strict group
ownership limits, which meant that national syndication
required negotiations with many independent station
owners. Broadcast operated under the FCC's fairness
doctrine, whose core requirements were that broadcasters cover matters of public importance and that they do
so fairly, mostly in the sense that they air competing positions. The doctrine was often associated with a right of
reply for politicians who were subject to personal attack
and other elements of the broader "public trustee" doctrine that held that private broadcasters holding licenses
to public airwaves should act in managing those airwaves
as a trustee for the real owners—the American people.
While the fairness doctrine did not often result in complete silencing, it made many broadcasters skittish about
airing programming that they thought might trigger an
obligation to grant free response time to those attacked
in these broadcasts.[23]

The 1987 FCC decision to stop enforcing the fairness doctrine supercharged conservative media into a billion-dollar
industry. Now there was no need to be concerned with offer-
ing equal time or performing a news function. It was true for
liberals and conservatives, but the conservative audience has
proven wider, more reliable, and more profitable, which is not
surprising. For all the reasons discussed above, conservatives
were hungry for a different source of information and belief,
a stronger bond than mere opinion, that would validate and

confirm their view of the world that was strikingly different from that presented by "mainstream" media. In 1988, Rush Limbaugh launched his radio show, and as Max Boot points out in *The Corrosion of Conservatism,* "Limbaugh called his fans 'dittoheads' because they mindlessly echoed his prejudices—or he theirs; the pandering went both ways."[24] Conservatives have managed to turn the phrase "mainstream media," or "lame stream media," as that noted arbiter of intellectual rigor, Sarah Palin, called it, into a pejorative. But what is mainstream media? It's the journalism that believes in standards, strives to report facts, and has a professional standard to correct errors. It's the news the majority of Americans consume. The brand of conservatism that has emerged from those early beginnings at *Human Events* requires the absence of professional standards. The entire purpose of this ever-increasing brand of conservative journalism—and it does great violence to the profession to call most of it by that term—is to confirm not just your opinion but also your *feelings.*

The charge that Barack Obama was not born in America is a quintessential conservative media moment, an attempt to provide some factual basis for bigotry. The birthers "felt" that a black man named Barack Hussein Obama could not truly be an American, so a cottage industry was born attempting to "prove" a lie. That it was demonstrably a lie backed by hospital records was quickly brushed aside in pursuit of the "larger" truth that Barack Obama wasn't "really" an American because an America that could elect a man with the middle name Hussein is not really America. The playing ground between "mainstream" media and the conservative alternatives is forever tilted against the side that has standards, because part of those standards is admitting mistakes and correcting them on the record. The result is a disproportionally long catalog of errors in the press with standards because, more often than not, there is little if any pressure within conservative journalism to admit errors, much less correct them. It happens every day, again and again, in large and small instances that combine to reinforce whatever it is that share of the conservative world chooses to believe.

The day I am writing this, Donald Trump, leading up to a visit to England, was asked about critical remarks made by Meghan Markle about Trump before she married Prince Harry. They included her support for Hillary Clinton, "not because she is a woman, but because Trump has made it easy to see that you don't really want that kind of world that he's painting." She also said that she might move to Canada if Trump was elected.[25]

Trump responded, "I didn't know that. What can I say? I didn't know that she was nasty." When his remarks drew criticism, Trump tweeted, "I never called Meghan Markle 'nasty.' Made up by the Fake News Media, and they caught cold! Will @CNN, @nytimes and others apologize? Doubt it!" As he was leaving for England, Trump insisted again, "No, I made no bad comments."[26]

The Trump era's consistent denial that you did not hear what you heard and did not see what you saw has managed to make George Orwell one of the most relevant authors of the day. When Donald Trump tweets, "What you're seeing and what you're reading is not what's happening," Orwell's *1984* is the perfect framework in which to understand his mentality: "The party told you to reject the evidence of your eyes and ears. It was their final, most essential command."[27]

There is an old joke about a country lawyer who, when he was hired to defend a man accused of killing a family of four and their dog, produces a dog and denies everything. When the Trump wing of the conservative media isn't simply inventing something out of nothing—the murder "conspiracy" of the DNC staffer Seth Rich is a perfect example—it loves to take one bit of truth and abuse it into a much larger lie. Some of this is merely silly and falls into the category of life imitating high school. But some has profound impact on domestic and foreign policy. When the Mueller Report was complete and did not find grounds sufficient to bring a charge of criminal conspiracy against the Trump campaign, it became for Trump "complete and total exoneration," and he immediately renewed his demand for an investigation into the "conspiracy" against him. Conspiracies are dominant realities in the world Trump and his followers inhabit. Unseen but powerful forces that the uninitiated can't see shape their world. Mollie Hemingway writes in *The Federalist*,

> I didn't fall for the Russia hoax that CNN and other media outlets did because I worked hard at understanding the appeal of his candidacy even before the Russia narrative started. At the same time, I recognized how disruptive he was to the established order and the livelihoods of those who had grown comfortable in D.C.

Unlike many reporters, I knew and loved many people who voted for Trump. My background as a media critic made me aware of information campaigns and how to resist them. My dislike of the interventionist foreign policy made me less susceptible to scaremongering about realist foreign policy.[28]

This is the language not of journalism in search of truth but of a cult. She had been trained in "information campaigns and how to resist them." Those information campaigns would be run by *The Wall Street Journal, USA Today, The New York Times, The Washington Post, The Atlanta Journal-Constitution,* ABC News, CBS News, NBC News . . . and, yes, CNN. It wasn't facts that led her to the conclusion but knowing "many people who voted for Trump," as if it were impossible that many good people could have voted for Donald Trump and been unaware that his campaign had been working with Russians. That you know and love people who voted for Trump only proves that you know and love people who voted for Trump. The irony of this is that while the Mueller Report did not charge Trump or his campaign with criminal conspiracy, it did uncover the largest effort in American history by a hostile foreign power to influence the selection of our commander in chief. That was the actual "information campaign," and it is a profound and deeply troubling revelation that is ignored by those eager to celebrate that Donald Trump was not indicted. The Russians' intelligence agents working through the blandly named Internet Research Agency (IRA) referred to their efforts as "information warfare." From the Mueller Report:

The IRA later used social media accounts and interest groups to sow discord in the U.S. political system through what it termed "information warfare." The campaign evolved from a generalized program designed in 2014 and 2015 to undermine the U.S. electoral system, to a targeted operation that by early 2016 favored candidate Trump and disparaged candidate Clinton. The IRA's operation also included the purchase of political advertisements on social media in the names of U.S. persons and entities, as well as the staging of political rallies inside the United States.[29]

In a sane world, a center-right party of a country facing an attack on the foundation of its democracy would lead the charge to defend the country. It was a Republican president, Ronald Reagan, who issued the ringing challenge to the Soviet Union "Mr. Gorbachev, tear down this wall." That party has now been transformed into Russian apologists, more concerned with defending Donald Trump than defending the country. It's madness. The modern Republican Party that has pushed the Pentagon budget to over $700 billion a year, that supports American military personnel in over 150 countries—those same Republicans have suddenly decided that Russian attacks don't matter because "our side" won.

Why? These are not stupid men and women, though more than a few do a fair imitation. They all will have their own justifications that amount to a personal Faustian bargain predicated on the self-delusion that some particular issue or cause is more important than their oath of office. But equally powerful will be the reinforcing group mentality that Congressman Justin Amash, the first and, as of this writing, the lone Republican congressman to call for Trump's impeachment, describes:

> My colleagues tell me all the time—in fact, you wouldn't believe how many phone conversations I've had, or conversations in person with colleagues. . . . A lot of them think I'm right about the Mueller Report. And they just won't say it. A lot of Republicans. What they'll say to me is, Justin, you know, going out publicly with that, you know the Democrats will never support you. You know that they're hypocrites on this stuff. And I say, you know, some of them are and some of them aren't. It doesn't matter to me. Because you have to look at what you're doing first. You have to care about what you're doing. If you have a society where all we care about is that the other side is bad, and therefore we don't have to do the right thing, that society will break down, and you will have no liberty. I refuse to be a part of that.[30]

The Republican Party is held aloft by a large, powerful, and ever-growing industry of deceit. The purpose of much of conservative media is to lie to their audience. It is fitting that at the heart of the Trump presidency itself is a lie: Almost every Republican elected official in Washington knows Donald Trump is unfit to be president. They knew it on November 9 at 7:00 p.m. when they were planning on how to rebuild the party from the disaster of nominating a know-nothing racist for president, and they knew it at midnight, when they were all frantically calling the oddballs and kooks Trump had assembled into a campaign to lavishly praise their brilliance. The Republican Party stood by a candidate who ran on a religious test to enter the United States. They knew it was unconstitutional and indecent, but they were silent. All through 2016, I had conversations with what passed for leadership in the Republican Party on the need to stand up to Trump. Most of their responses went like this: "Trump is a disaster and a disgrace. But we have to let him lose on his own. If we, the establishment, put our thumbs on the scale, when he loses it will be our fault and not the fault of his racism, the alt-right, and those idiots at Breitbart. We will have elected Hillary Clinton. We have to let him lose and rebuild."

To which I always responded, "But what if he wins?" Truth was, though, I didn't think he would win, and I wasn't great at making the case for something I didn't believe. What these Republican leaders were saying wasn't crazy; it just proved to be wrong. And in that miscalculation began the surrender of any sense of self to Donald Trump. So now the nation is in full possession of the reality that Russians—Russians, for cryin' out loud—worked on the same side as every Republican volunteer, donor, elected official, and Trump voter. When you learn that the bank you borrowed money from is actually owned by a drug cartel, should your first reaction be, "Well, we got a good interest rate"? The simple reality is that the Republican Party was in business with Russian intelligence efforts, what used to be known as the KGB, and precious few leading the Republican Party seem to give a damn.

I've spent decades waking up every morning eager to fight

Democrats, trying to gain every bit of advantage for every battle. God knows we made mistakes and played too often on the dark side. But I never woke up knowing that somewhere out there a Russian agent was waking up with the same job I had.

My dad was in the FBI when Hoover ordered the roundup of Asian Americans. He hated it and quit, joined the navy, and spent the next three years fighting in the South Pacific. Like so many, he didn't talk a lot about the war. But when it came to leaving the FBI, he told me once, "You can always say no."

And that's my question to all those Republicans who are more worried about defending Donald Trump than defending America: Is this why you went into politics? Is this why you put up with all the bullshit and stupidity that is integral to our political system, so you can be on the same side as the Russians?

You can always say no. I so wish Republican leaders would try it.

6

WHAT ARE THEY
AFRAID OF?

Every critic, every detractor, will have to bow down to President Trump.

—Omarosa Manigault[1]

The most distinguishing characteristic of the current national Republican Party is cowardice. The base price of admission is a willingness to accept that an unstable, pathological liar leads it and pretend otherwise. This means the party demands dishonesty as a trait of membership—unless you are a rare sociopath who defends pathological lying. They do exist. The vast majority of Republican elected officials know Donald Trump is unfit to be president and pretend otherwise.

Among Trump critics, it is often said that the Republican leaders lack the courage to stand up to Donald Trump. But even that analysis is flattering to Republicans. Courage is not standing up to a ludicrous man-child like Donald Trump. Courage is getting out of the boat when the soldier in front of you was just killed. That's the legacy of the current generation of our politicians, and while there is failure of courage enough to go around across the political spectrum, my brief is the Republican Party and its total collapse as a moral force.

Degree matters, and it is much easier to see a flawed Democratic Party at least attempting to hold to some semblance of its long-espoused values than the Republican Party tying itself in knots trying to justify a man they know is unqualified. If the Republican Party had been in charge in 1776, we'd all still be celebrating the queen's birthday. They would have timidly said, "What are we going to do, fight England? Fight the king? The most powerful army in the world?" and then set about to negotiate how much of their dignity they could pretend to keep in a pathetic effort to please. Cowardice is one of the least appealing of human qualities, and a deeply damaged Cowardly Lion leads the Republican Party. To willingly follow a coward against your own values and to put your own power above the good of the nation is to become a coward.

Parties and elected officials don't suddenly wake up one day and decide to betray avowed principles. It's a gradual process of surrendering little bits of your soul and values while convincing yourself it is for a greater good. Rationalization is like a lot of things in life: the more you do it, the easier it becomes. The story of Faust is not just that Mephistopheles takes your soul; he also doesn't deliver on what he promised. Cowardice, like courage, is contagious, and to be surrounded by cowards is to feel comforted in the knowledge that not only are there others like you but there is probably someone worse. The American political process with its deep dependence on the need to raise money is a system designed not for the best governance but for the selection of the person who can put up with being humiliated the longest. Those with the lowest standards willing to grovel and beg are often the recipients of the greatest rewards. That's true across any party lines, but what is unique about the Republican Party is the clear direction in which it has allowed itself to be driven.

Special interest groups are like terrorists: they test for weakness and exploit fear. What happened to the Republican Party is that slowly over half a century the kooks and weirdos and social misfits of a conservative ideology started discovering that they could force reasonable people to support unreasonable positions through fear. The transition of the National Rifle Association is a perfect parable: over a couple of decades, it evolved from a gun-safety education organization to a thuggish gang that rewards those at the top with millions of dollars based on proven ability to muscle elected officials into doing what they mostly know is wrong. Today the leaders of the Republican Party follow Donald Trump's lead and routinely attack the foundations of law enforcement, from the FBI to the Justice Department to the judiciary. At first glance it seems stunning to witness a party that once defined itself as a "law-and-order party" take the same position as every drug dealer, child pornographer, Mafia don, and human trafficker who claims innocence and attacks government officials for unfair tactics. Like another guy who lived in Queens named John Gotti, Donald Trump calls criminals who tell the truth "rats" and uses a deep bench of corrupt and compromised lawyers like Rudy Giuliani to plead his case in public and rally support against law enforcement for doing their jobs.

Shocking as it seems to hear the White House sound like a recording from the famed Mafia hangout the Ravenite Social Club in Little Italy, the precedent for the Republican Party's attacking law enforcement has been established for decades by the National Rifle Association. In 1995, the head of the NRA, Wayne LaPierre, attacked a federal assault weapons ban for giving "jack-booted government thugs more power to take away our constitutional rights, break in our doors, seize our guns, destroy our property, and even injure or kill us." Under President Bill Clinton, LaPierre charged, "if you have a badge, you have the government's go-ahead to harass, intimidate, even murder law-abiding citizens." This is the sort of language used by any homegrown terrorist group, from neo-Nazis to the 1960s radical-left bombers of the Students for a Democratic Society.[2] That was enough to make President George H. W. Bush resign his lifetime NRA membership in a blistering letter. It's worth reading the whole text to get a sense of the totality of Bush's fury:

I was outraged when, even in the wake of the Oklahoma City tragedy, Mr. Wayne LaPierre, executive vice president of N.R.A., defended his attack on federal agents as "jack-booted thugs." To attack Secret Service agents or A.T.F. people or any government law enforcement people as "wearing Nazi bucket helmets and black storm trooper uniforms" wanting to "attack law abiding citizens" is a vicious slander on good people.

Al Whicher, who served on my [U.S. Secret Service] detail when I was Vice President and President, was killed in Oklahoma City. He was no Nazi. He was a kind man, a loving parent, a man dedicated to serving his country—and serve it well he did.

In 1993, I attended the wake for A.T.F. agent Steve

Willis, another dedicated officer who did his duty. I can assure you that this honorable man, killed by weird cultists, was no Nazi.

John Magaw, who used to head the U.S.S.S. and now heads A.T.F., is one of the most principled, decent men I have ever known. He would be the last to condone the kind of illegal behavior your ugly letter charges. The same is true for the F.B.I.'s able Director Louis Freeh. I appointed Mr. Freeh to the Federal Bench. His integrity and honor are beyond question.

Both John Magaw and Judge Freeh were in office when I was President. They both now serve in the current administration. They both have badges. Neither of them would ever give the government's "go ahead to harass, intimidate, even murder law abiding citizens." (Your words) I am a gun owner and an avid hunter. Over the years I have agreed with most of N.R.A.'s objectives, particularly your educational and training efforts, and your fundamental stance in favor of owning guns.

However, your broadside against Federal agents deeply offends my own sense of decency and honor; and it offends my concept of service to country. It indirectly slanders a wide array of government law enforcement officials, who are out there, day and night, laying their lives on the line for all of us.

You have not repudiated Mr. LaPierre's unwarranted attack. Therefore, I resign as a Life Member of N.R.A., said resignation to be effective upon your receipt of this letter. Please remove my name from your membership list. Sincerely, [signed] George Bush[3]

In 1994, I was working on the campaign of the then congressman Tom Ridge, who was running for governor of Pennsylvania. Ridge was from Erie, and when he announced, a prominent political columnist for the *Philadelphia Daily News* called Ridge "the man no one had ever heard of from the city no one had ever seen." He started out toward the bottom in a field of five running for the Republican nomination. He'd been the first to graduate from college in his family, went to Harvard on a scholarship, and, when drafted, went to Vietnam as a grunt, one of the few college graduates who chose not to seek an officer's commission. It was a hard, complicated race, and two weeks before the primary four candidates had a shot to win.

A week before the Republican primary, a long-debated bill to ban assault weapons came up for a vote in Congress. For a Republican running in a primary, the obvious and easy answer was to vote against it. James Carville once described Pennsylvania as Philadelphia to the east, Pittsburgh to the west, and Alabama in the middle. I remember well a tense conference call when the campaign pollster went through the likely fallout of supporting the ban, and it was all bad, no upside. Ridge had been a prosecutor in Erie and was familiar, like everyone who worked in law enforcement, with the terrible consequences of gun violence. Ridge listened to the numbers and didn't hesitate: "I'm voting for it. If I lose, I lose. Screw 'em." Only thirty-eight Republicans voted for it, and it passed by two votes. A week later, Ridge won the primary. Then he went on to win the general election and is the last Republican in Pennsylvania to have been reelected as governor.

The same November day when Tom Ridge won the Pennsylvania governorship, Republicans took control of Congress for the first time in fifty years. This was the "Contract with America" election that made Newt Gingrich into the Death Star of the Republican Party. No single political figure better illustrates the predicate for Donald Trump than Newt Gingrich. Both men are deeply damaged psychological cripples from dysfunctional families. In *The Atlantic*, McKay Coppins described Gingrich's stepfather as "a brooding, violent man who showed little affection for 'Newtie,' the pudgy, flat-footed, bookish boy his wife had foisted upon him." His mother "struggled with manic depression, and spent much of her adult life in a fog of medication."[4] Donald Trump's relationship to his family is so tortured he has the bizarre need to reinvent their origins, claiming in *Trump: The Art of the Deal* that his grandfather came to America "from Sweden as a child."[5] Then, in 2019, he claimed his father was born in Germany. Trump tried to temper his complaints about Germany's not paying enough to NATO by saying, "I have great respect for Angela [Merkel] and I have great respect for the country. My father is German, was German, born in a very wonderful place in Germany so I have a very great feeling for Germany."[6] Trump's father was actually born in New York and his grandfather in Germany.[7] Both Trump and Gingrich have a transparent need to compensate for their deep insecurities with childlike boasting. Coppins summed up Gingrich's sense of self-grandeur:

> He has described himself as a "transformational figure" and "the most serious, systematic revolutionary of modern times." To one reporter, he declared, "I want to

shift the entire planet. And I'm doing it." To another, he said, "People like me are what stand between us and Auschwitz."[8]

Like Trump, Gingrich spent decades in the pursuit of what he considered "trading up" in wives, starting with his high school geometry teacher and ending up, as of this writing, with a former intern he was having sex with while leading the impeachment against Bill Clinton for lying about having sex with an intern. That the former House intern, Callista Gingrich, is now the American ambassador to the Vatican is further evidence both that irony is dead and that God has a sense of humor. In most normalized societies, Newt Gingrich and Donald Trump would be considered nonserious comic figures to be pitied if in a charitable mood and mocked if less generous. Both are total frauds at their self-described identities. As has been observed, Newt Gingrich is a dumb person's idea of a smart person, and Donald Trump is a not-rich person's idea of wealth. It says a lot about the Republican Party that both of these disturbed and broken men have become dominant figures. Their unifying thread is anger at a world that has treated them far more generously than they deserved.

When Tom Ridge voted in support of the assault weapons ban in 1994, joining him were Bob Michel, the Republican minority leader, and one of the House's conservative leaders, Henry Hyde of Illinois, most known for his opposition to abortion. (The Hyde Amendment, passed in 1976, banned the use of federal funds for all abortions except in cases of rape or incest or to protect the life of the mother.) While thirty-eight

Republicans voted for the assault weapons ban, seventy-seven Democrats voted against it, which accurately reflects the less polarized nature of Washington back then. Gingrich, of course, voted against it. As Republicans challenged Democrats for control of Congress, polarization increased. Interesting work has been done that suggests American political parties become more polarized as equal competition between the parties increases. The political science professor Frances Lee at the University of Maryland wrote in *The Washington Post*,

> Competition fuels party conflict by raising the political stakes of every policy dispute. When control of national institutions hangs in the balance, no party wants to grant political legitimacy to its opposition by voting for the measures it champions. After all, how can a party wage an effective campaign after supporting or collaborating with its opposition on public policy? Instead, parties in a competitive environment will want to amplify the differences voters perceive between themselves and their opposition.[9]

It makes sense. The Princeton political science professor Nolan McCarty has written extensively on polarization and has come to a similar conclusion on the toxic mix of competition for control of Congress and the inability for a government to govern:

> Polarization in Congress derives from both sincere ideological differences about policy means and ends and

strategic behavior to exploit those differences to win elections. The combination of high ideological stakes and intense competition for party control of the national government has all but eliminated the incentives for significant bipartisan cooperation on important national problems. Consequently, polarization has reduced congressional capacity to govern.[10]

It isn't unusual to see both parties blamed for the dysfunction in Washington, which is one of those generalities that fall into a useless-truth category. Yes, both parties are to blame, but here is the actual relevant question to ask: Is one party more to blame than the other? Professor McCarty is clear on Republicans' greater role in the negativity of polarization:

The evidence points to a major partisan asymmetry in polarization. Despite the widespread belief that both parties have moved to the extremes, the movement of the Republican Party to the right accounts for most of the divergence between the two parties. Since the 1970s, each new cohort of Republican legislators has taken more conservative positions on legislation than the cohorts before them. That is not true of Democratic legislators.[11]

Looking back at the thirty-eight Republicans in the House of Representatives who voted for the 1994 assault weapons ban is like stumbling across artifacts of a long-lost civilization. These elements of the party were always a minority, but their existence and acceptance allowed the party to at least pretend it was a tolerant big-tent party with a divergence of ideology. It was obvious since 1964 that "moderates"—a flexible characterization that is graded on the curve of the moment's politics—would not be dominant in the party, but when there were prominent elected officials who were pro-choice, supported gun control like the assault weapons ban, spoke out convincingly on civil rights, and were committed to governing victories over ideological defeats, it altered the perception of the party. That has all changed. Today most of the thirty-eight Republicans who supported the assault weapons ban would have little place in the Republican Party. Joe McDade from Pennsylvania's Tenth Congressional District was one of seven Republicans who signed a telegram in 1966 to Georgia's governor, Carl Sanders, after the Georgia General Assembly refused to seat the black antiwar activist and civil rights leader Julian Bond. The telegram called the refusal "a dangerous attack on representative government. None of us agree with Mr. Bond's views on the Vietnam War; in fact we strongly repudiate those views. But unless otherwise determined by a court of law, which the Georgia Legislature is not, he is entitled to express them."[12]

Compare this with today's Republican Party that chants "Lock her/him up" about political opponents. Congresswoman Deborah Pryce from Columbus, Ohio, was a member of the Republican Majority for Choice and Republicans for Environmental Protection. The seat is now held by Steve Stivers, who has an A rating from the NRA, has voted for abortion bans, and reaffirmed his endorsement of Donald Trump after the *Access Hollywood* tape in which Trump bragged of assaulting women. The Sierra Club endorsed Congressman Jim Saxton from New Jersey's Third District. A Democrat, Andy Kim, who was a Rhodes scholar and endorsed by President Obama, now holds that seat. In Massachusetts, Peter Blute, who supported the assault weapons ban, was defeated two years later by the Democrat Jim McGovern, and only one Republican, Scott Brown, has won a House or Senate race in Massachusetts since Blute. (I worked for Governor Bill Weld when he ran against John Kerry in 1996; we lost.)

From the Eastern Shore of Maryland, the Republican Wayne Gilchrest supported some abortion rights, was the only Republican to support D.C. statehood, and was co-chairman of the Congressional Climate Change Caucus. (Unimaginable now.) He was defeated in the 2008 Republican primary by a right-winger who then lost the general election. In Iowa, Congressman Jim Leach was a Princeton and Johns Hopkins graduate, a former Foreign Service officer, and pro-choice, and he served as president of the largest international association of legislators, Parliamentarians for Global Action. That was before Republicans decided "globalists" was a code word for some shadowy international cabal of Jewish bankers. In his 2006 reelection, Leach refused to let the Republican National Committee attack his Democratic opponent Dave Loebsack for supporting gay marriage, and he lost a close race. Loebsack continues to hold the seat.

These thirty-eight who stood up to the NRA belonged to a Republican Party that no longer exists. In 2011, Mike Lofgren ended a twenty-eight year career as one of the most respected Republican budget experts and staffers on Capitol Hill when he left the Republican Party in disgust. In his career, Lofgren had witnessed the transformation of the Republican Party from a party that at least pretended to serve a competent governing duty to a well-funded collection of political warriors with no greater purpose than staying in power. As he wrote in *The Party Is Over: How Republicans Went Crazy, Democrats Became Useless, and the Middle Class Got Shafted*, "When I came to Washington in the early 1980s, the GOP was the 'party of ideas' and seemed on the verge of becoming the dominant political factor on the American scene."[13] He summed up the change embodied in the insanity of the government shutdown in 2011 over the passage of a simple bill to extend the national debt ceiling and stop the government from default:

> To those millions of Americans who watched with exasperation the tragicomedy of summer 2011's debt-ceiling extension crisis, it might have come as a shock that the Republican Party is so full of lunatics. To be sure, like any political party on Earth, the GOP has always had its share of crackpots, such as Robert K. Dornan or William E. Dannemeyer in past Congresses. But the crackpot outliers of two decades ago have become the vital core today: Eric Cantor, Steve King, Michele Bachmann, Paul Broun, Patrick McHenry, Virginia Foxx, Louie Gohmert, and Allen West. The *Congressional Directory* now reads like a casebook of lunacy.[14]

That was in 2011, or the pre-Trump era that is now considered "the good ole days." Writing years before Trump supposedly "hijacked" the Republican Party from its higher purpose, Lofgren explained perfectly the conditions that made a Donald Trump not a freak by-product of a flawed Electoral College but an inevitable next step on the path chosen by Republicans:

> The GOP has been gradually shedding its status as a broad coalition party and has started demanding litmus tests on fiscal, social, and foreign policy issues. There were signposts on the road ahead—the Gingrich revolution of 1995, the Clinton impeachment circus—but things got much worse after September 11, with the massive infringements of civil liberties that followed and the bluster and bravado that preceded the invasion of Iraq. By the 2010 midterm election the party had collectively lost its mind. The evidence is all around us: the debt ceiling debacle, the kamikaze politics over the payroll tax cut extension, the freak show of the Republican presidential debates.

When Tom Ridge was facing a decision on how to vote on the 1994 assault weapons ban, I'd like to say I urged him to vote for the ban, that I channeled my inner Jimmy Stewart in *Mr. Smith Goes to Washington* and urged him to do what would make the Boy Rangers proud. I didn't, nor did I advise him to vote against it. I never thought my role was to remind clients of their deeply held beliefs. But I know I was hoping he would vote against it. I cared about one thing—winning—and had every reason to believe it would mean we'd lose.

(Six years later, I was jogging in Crawford, Texas, with Governor Bush during the time when he was considering whom to pick as vice president. It was the middle of the day, well over a hundred degrees, and we were sweating so much it felt more like swimming than running. "Governor," I asked, "would it be appropriate for me to make a suggestion on the VP?" Without missing a step or looking at me, Bush said, "Hell no. Why the hell would I care what you think?" We were running with Mark McKinnon, and he came close to falling down into the scrub grass laughing. Later, Governor Bush said to me, "Stevens, let me get you some advice. When a guy is getting married, wait until he asks what you think of his fiancée before you tell him." It did seem like very good advice. If given the chance, I was going to push Governor Ridge.)

Looking back, I often think I represented the worst of the American political system, just focused on winning without regard for the consequences. That I stumbled into a profession which considered only winning an acceptable ethical code might serve as a convenient excuse, but it was hardly a justification. Of those congressmen who voted against the assault weapons ban, it would be foolishly disingenuous to assert that each did so for political reasons. It's fair to say that many believed it was the right vote based on their principles. But few of those who supported the NRA position opposing the assault weapons ban would agree with the extreme attacks on law enforcement, calling those who put their lives on the line defending Americans "jack-booted thugs." But only a handful had the courage to take the step President George H. W. Bush took in resigning from the NRA.

The negative effects of special interest money on our politics are often blamed for much of the collapse of governance. In *So Damn Much Money,* the *Washington Post* reporter Robert Kaiser traced the impact of money, using the example of the 2006 conviction of the Republican lobbyist and former head of the College Republicans Jack Abramoff as a parable of the corruption of money in politics:

> In a debate on campaign finance reform in 1971, one of the lions of the Senate, Russell B. Long, observed that "the distinction between a campaign contribution and a bribe is almost a hairline's difference. You can hardly tell one from the other." Long spoke at a time when candidates for the House and Senate raised tens or hundreds of thousands to run campaigns every two or six years. A generation later, when Abramoff got into trouble, members of the House and Senate raised millions, or tens of millions, to wage their re-election campaigns. They routinely spent a fourth or a third of their working hours soliciting those campaign contributions that Long and Abramoff both thought looked a great deal like bribes.[15]

As a high-level congressional staffer for decades, Mike Lofgren had a close view of the corruption of our campaign finance system:

> The police and petty bureaucrats in many Third World countries are openly corrupt and will take bribes in order to augment their miserable salaries. In the United

States it is relatively difficult to bribe a cop to get out of a traffic ticket or to slip money to a DMV functionary to get preferential treatment. You need to go higher up the governmental food chain in order to practice corruption successfully. But you can find bribery and corruption just about anytime, year-round, in Washington. It is called a fund-raiser, when a congress member's campaign committee rents a room in a restaurant and invites a hundred or so of his or her closest friends from the lobbying shops on K Street, from industry, and from the trade associations. I've been to a few of these over the years and often wondered whether any of the Gucci-shod participants in their two-thousand-dollar suits and monogrammed shirts imagined that they were righteously engaged in the constitutional practice of petitioning for the redress of grievances as they handed over their checks before tucking into the hors d'oeuvres.[16]

I've become a radical on campaign finance and support a system of federal funding for all elections. It seems to be forgotten these days, but one of the key post-Watergate reforms was a system of federal funding for presidential elections. Under the system, each candidate received around $80 million—it went up every four years—in exchange for agreeing to not raise or spend more money. The check was presented to the campaign when the candidate finished giving his acceptance speech at the national convention. (It was always a check; invariably we'd ask if the money could be wired to a campaign account, and the answer was always,

"No, we do checks.") This system was why, in the Bush campaign, we pushed the 2004 convention to as late as possible. The law stipulated it had to be accepted no later than sixty days before the election; it dawned on us that we'd get the same amount of money at the end of August as in June or July, and there'd be an advantage to concentrating the amount in a shorter period of time.

Every presidential candidate stuck to that system until 2008, when Barack Obama, after routinely pledging to accept federal funding, realized how much money he could raise and decided to reject federal funding. John McCain stayed in the system with the result that he had $83 million for his campaign and Obama had more than $300 million for his. As is always the case with campaign finance reforms, once the system was broken, it proved impossible to put the genie back in the bottle, and subsequent candidates rejected public funding. Today some defend the decision by then senator Obama to blow up the system, insisting it was necessary to cope with the large amount of money Republicans could raise after the *Citizens United* Supreme Court decision that allowed contributions from corporations to be treated the same as individual donations—an explanation that makes no sense, because the ruling was two years after the 2008 campaign. The ending of the federal funding system is, in my view, one of the most negative long-term legacies of the Obama administration.

Money and the necessity of its craven pursuit have polluted and twisted our elections in destructive ways that all reduce the power of the individual, distorting the essence of democracy in ways unimaginable even fifty years ago. But it isn't really the power of money that gave right-wing special interests so much power over Republican politicians; it's the ability of those groups to mobilize voters. A candidate can always raise more money from different sources. An infinite amount of money is available to candidates who are willing to do the demeaning work of fund-raising and have a message that motivates some segments of the electorate. But there are a finite number of voters in every election. Both parties have a vast array of special interests, from the NRA to labor unions, that have the ability to mobilize voters to support or oppose their choice of candidates. The difference between the impact of these groups on each party goes to the fundamental asymmetrical structures of the parties. The modern Democratic Party is a much more diverse, heterogeneous association of voters. By definition it is more difficult for one group to have like influence over female African Americans (the voters who defeated Roy Moore in Alabama), college-educated men, Hispanics who speak Spanish at home, and urban young voters. The core groups that influence the Democratic nominating process the most are African Americans, labor, and liberals. These are wildly disparate voters with different, sometimes competing interests.

Compare that with the overwhelming majority of Republican voters, who are white, Christian, and middle class or more affluent. The NRA has made it impossible for a Republican to oppose their group—not because of their funding, but because of their base of supporters who can be mobilized in Republican primaries. It is near functionally impossible for a Republican to win a presidential nomination in the Republican

Party and actively oppose the NRA. That places the NRA as gatekeepers to the power center of the Republican Party. The only like group in the Democratic Party would be the coalition of groups who support pro-choice candidates. They are matched in the Republican Party by opponents to abortion, with the result that unlike twenty or more years ago, when there were pro-choice Republican senators and a sprinkling of anti-abortion Democratic senators, the two parties on the federal level now represent opposing views on abortion.

On economic issues, one man, Grover Norquist, has spent the last thirty years pressuring Republican candidates to commit to a pledge not to raise taxes. His group, Americans for Tax Reform, and his antitax cause have become so ubiquitous that Republican politicians and operatives refer to "the pledge," as in "have you signed the pledge?" No other explanation is needed. Norquist has acquired disproportionate power because, if there is one single unifying conviction among Republicans, it is the assumption that all good in government flows from cutting taxes.

There is no like unanimity among the coalition of the Democratic Party. In 2008, Barack Obama raised more money from the financial industry—that's shorthand for really rich, mostly white people—than any candidate in American history. (In 2012, Mitt Romney raised more.) But Obama also received a record number of African American votes. (Actually, he received more votes in 2008 than any presidential candidate in American history.) Ask a hedge-fund Obama donor his or her view on taxes, and you'll likely get a different answer from that of a sixty-five-year-old teacher who donated to Obama.

Ask a Republican hedge-fund donor his or her view on taxes, and it is likely to be very similar to the response of a sixty-five-year-old Republican teacher.

The truth is that most Republican politicians I've known—and I've known a lot—greatly resent the power of Grover Norquist and resent the childlike indignity of signing a pledge, as if running for office were like joining some secret college society with rules. Most Republican politicians are not stupid and are aware on some level that committing to not raising taxes for the entirety of their careers greatly limits their and their party's basic ability to govern and deal with a chaotic and unpredictable world. Some indeed refuse to sign the pledge. But few if any Republican politicians will even broach the possibility of a tax increase. The result of this weakness will be generations forced to pay off the debt and interest resulting from the simpleminded conspiracy of silence that is a central tenet of Republican politics. It is as if nineteenth-century doctors were aware that leeches will not save their patients but would rather let them die than break the code of orthodoxy. There is a direct line between the rising of the national debt and the increased influence of Grover Norquist and Americans for Tax Reform. The Republican Party is the frog carrying the scorpion of Grover Norquist across the river.

America is a big, diverse, loud, contradictory country and getting more so every hour. Today more than forty-four million Americans were born in another country, the highest percentage since 1910. As much as Donald Trump might desire, precious few of those are coming from Scandinavia, and even fewer are models from eastern Europe, his favorite hunting grounds for spouses and girlfriends. The largest group is Mexicans, and the second largest is from India. Non-Mexican South Americans are the third-largest group. Donald Trump—and that means the Republican Party—has attacked Mexicans as "rapists," and he rants every few weeks about an invasion from South America, as if the Chilean military had just landed in San Diego and were broadcasting live from SeaWorld. Trump hasn't gone out of his way to attack immigrants from India, at least not as of this writing, but they get the joke. In the 2016 presidential election, 62 percent of Indian American voters had an unfavorable view of Trump versus 65 percent favorable for the Democratic Party. President Barack Obama had an 83 percent favorable.[17]

The power a small group of right-wing zealots has over the Republican Party will continue until one of two events occurs: either a critical mass of Republican politicians stands together and stands up to their power, or the party changes such that it is not a white party but a party that looks more like America. As a point of reference, at some point in the future the sun will collapse as a red star and consume the earth. I'd call it a toss-up as to which of these three events is likely to happen first.

7

THE ANTI-AMERICAN PATRIOTS

It became necessary to destroy the town to save it.
—Unnamed Major, United States Army,
February 7, 1968, press briefing

In the 2016 election, Donald Trump consistently benefited from the inability to imagine him winning. That belief shaped the Republican primary. The driving dynamic for the primary was the competition between the non-Trump candidates to narrow the race to one on one with Trump. It seemed obvious that the Republican Party would not nominate someone who was a bankrupt casino owner who lost the Reform Party nomination for president to Pat Buchanan in 2000, was a maxed-out donor to Anthony Weiner, had attacked Republicans for being against abortion, had bragged that his building was now the tallest after the Twin Towers collapsed on 9/11, and who talked longingly in public about dating his daughter.[1] The notion was absurd. So the real race was to beat every candidate whose last name wasn't Trump, and then the last stage, just beating Trump, would be an easy layup.

Likewise in the general election, the "inevitability" of

Hillary Clinton might very well have sealed her fate. James Comey, FBI director at the time of the election, has said that the assumption of a Clinton victory prompted his release of his infamous letter revealing that the FBI was investigating a newly acquired batch of Clinton-related emails. In his book, *A Higher Loyalty*, Comey wrote, "Assuming, as nearly everyone did, that Hillary Clinton would be elected president of the United States in less than two weeks, what would happen to the FBI, the Justice Department, or her own presidency if it later was revealed, after the fact, that she was still a subject of an FBI investigation?"[2] For most of the 2016 general election, Trump was losing college-educated voters (which is very close to saying "college-educated white Republican voters"). No Republican nominee had lost this group in modern history. Even *Goldwater* won college-educated Republicans in 1964. Until the release of the Comey letter, Trump was losing that group. There is no hard data that proves X percent of the electorate cast their vote as a protest vote not expecting the candidate to win—the methodology of such polling would be inherently flawed—but it's my view that a certain, not small, share of the electorate voted for Trump not really believing he would win. It's always best to be skeptical of such non-data-backed conclusions, but it does seem clear that the media coverage of Trump was more as a phenomenon or, in the beginning, a joke than as a potential presidential candidate. In a primary debate, Hugh Hewitt asked Trump, "What's your priority among our nuclear triad?"

Trump managed an answer that began with his standard

lie that he was against the Iraq war and ended with a bizarre assertion that World War II had been fought "hand to hand."

Hewitt looked on, puzzled, and asked a more specific question: "Of the three legs of the triad, though, do you have a priority?"

This time, Trump responded, "I think—I think, for me, nuclear is just the power, the devastation is very important to me," which made it painfully apparent that the guy who was running for the job to hold the nuclear codes didn't have a clue about the most fundamental basics of the deterrent strategy at the core of America's nuclear weapons arsenal.[3] It's difficult to think of a more disqualifying answer for a potential president. In the most charitable construct, let's imagine that Donald Trump just hadn't really considered himself a serious candidate in those early primary debates and surely, once he was the nominee, he would do whatever was necessary to become knowledgeable about the most serious obligation of a president. But nope, debating Hillary Clinton in September, he was still completely clueless about nuclear weapons, managing to say that America should never use nuclear weapons as a first strike and "we shouldn't take anything off the table" in the same answer. As Josh Rogin wrote in *The Washington Post,* "Trump's lack of basic understanding about nuclear weapons policy is concerning enough. But even more troubling is Trump's lack of progress over the past few months on national security issues overall. He simply refuses to make the effort to prepare himself for the job of commander in chief."[4]

That a national party once largely defined by its seriousness of intent in international affairs would be led by a man who not only was ignorant of the basics of national security but was willfully and unflinchingly proud of his ignorance is just one more milepost marking the journey of Republicans on their way to the junkyard of history. A strong stench of denial hovers around Donald Trump. I know; I was in deep denial that he could win the nomination of a party I'd worked for and the presidency of a country I love. For many who didn't particularly like Trump but couldn't bring themselves to vote for Hillary Clinton, there was the denial that Trump would be, as president, the same man he had been his entire life. At least I didn't fall for that one. It seemed obvious that Trump as president would continue to be the same badly damaged, semiliterate, incurious, and maladjusted oddball he had always been. If you know a woman who is marrying a man who is over seventy and she says there are a lot of things she doesn't like about him but she thinks he will change, what would you tell that woman? But many Republicans I know were convinced there was something mystical about Trump walking into the Oval Office that would elevate him. Normal people tend to believe that anyone acting abnormally will eventually revert to normalcy. Trump realizes this and has manipulated that mistaken belief of the normal—the marks and cons and suckers he has cheated and lied to his entire life—to great advantage.

In the spring of 2016 when it became apparent that Donald Trump was going to be the Republican nominee, I approached a number of individuals encouraging them to run as a "favorite son" candidate in their home states. The idea was simple: if a third-party candidate with an appeal to the center right ran and took votes from Trump, it would block his path to victory. I spoke to each person under strict confidentiality and so will not reveal names or states, but they were high-profile conservatives who believed that Trump was a disaster for the party and it would be better to lose one election than lose the moral mandate of a conservative movement. Each person was very sympathetic, but each argued that Trump was going to lose anyway and it was better for him to lose because he had terrible ideas and was morally bankrupt than because of the political mechanism of a third party draining votes. I argued there was still a danger he could win, but I probably wasn't very good at it, because I didn't really think he would win. We were all in denial.

The same sense of denial is at work whenever the "post-Trump" conservative movement is discussed. There is this desperate need to believe that having, as Ted Cruz called him, a "pathological liar" leading the center-right party of America will simply be selectively remembered. Like so much in our politics and popular culture—and it is difficult to separate the two—the race to extremes makes it difficult to discuss calmly and rationally the threat Donald Trump and the collapse of any moral center in the Republican Party present to our democratic process.[5] There is the standard warning that it is impossible to compare any contemporary moment to the events that led to World War II, but to deny those lessons and warnings of history is a grave mistake. At the end of Trump's first year in office, I found myself darkly joking that it was crazy to compare 2018 to 1932 when it was so obviously 1934. But Steven Levitsky and Daniel Ziblatt write in *How Democracies Die,*

> During the Cold War, coups d'état accounted for nearly three out of every four democratic breakdowns. Democracies in Argentina, Brazil, the Dominican Republic, Ghana, Greece, Guatemala, Nigeria, Pakistan, Peru, Thailand, Turkey, and Uruguay all died this way. More recently, military coups toppled Egyptian President Mohamed Morsi in 2013 and Thai Prime Minister Yingluck Shinawatra in 2014. In all these cases, democracy dissolved in spectacular fashion, through military power and coercion.
>
> But there is another way to break a democracy. It is less dramatic but equally destructive. Democracies may die at the hands not of generals but of elected leaders—presidents or prime ministers who subvert the very process that brought them to power. Some of these leaders dismantle democracy quickly, as Hitler did in the wake of the 1933 Reichstag fire in Germany. More often, though, democracies erode slowly, in barely visible steps.[6]

Republicans want what they perceive as the benefits of Donald Trump without the responsibility of supporting Trump. In this way, as in many, the ghost of Franz von Papen haunts today's GOP. If I could make every Republican elected official read one book, it would be the memoirs of Papen, the aristocratic chancellor of Germany who dissolved the German parliament and enabled Adolf Hitler to rise to power. Published in 1952, the *Memoirs of Franz von Papen* is a study in self-deception by an intelligent man who knows he made terrible mistakes with horrific consequences but is still trying to explain that his choices were the best of bad ones available. In an effort to justify abolishing the ban on Nazi storm troopers, he blamed left-wing radicals:

> It may well be asked why it was found necessary in a civilized state for political parties to organize these "protection forces." The answer is simple. In Britain or the United States the police forces protect the activities of every political party. In the Weimar Republic things were different. Right wing meetings were continually broken up and interrupted by left wing radicals. The police, most of whom came under Socialist Ministers of the Interior in the States, did not or would not do anything about it.
>
> The parties of the left pretended then, and continue to do so now, that the lifting of the ban on the Brownshirts was the first step in my hoisting the Nazis into the saddle. I have no doubt they find it convenient to look for a scapegoat. All that had happened was that equal rights for all parties, including both the Nazis and the Communists, had been restored. At any rate, this lasted only for a month.[7]

This is not an analogy of Trump to Adolf Hitler or the chanting of "Lock her up!" by the Trump faithful to the Brownshirts, but it is a cautionary warning on the collapse of norms in a society. Legitimizing hate is like a war: it is easier to begin than to stop. If there is any one single truth that binds together the varying concepts of conservatism, it must be about the nature of *conserving* that which is essential to a civil society. This one simplistic, unifying thread seems all the more critical because, as George Nash wrote in *The Conservative Intellectual Movement in America Since 1945,* "I offer here no compact definition of conservatism. In fact, American conservatives themselves have had no such agreed-upon definition. Instead, the very quest for self-definition has been one of the most notable motifs of their thought since World War II."[8] But popular perception is not unimportant, and the idea of "conserving" unites William Buckley's famous definition, using Papen's words, "by a stroke of the pen . . . the Chancellor possesses powers accorded not even to the German Kaisers" with Trump's campaign slogan, "Make America Great Again."[9] Both assume that a society is threatening to spin out of control or, at the very least, speeding toward an unknown and dangerous destination that compels true patriots, that is, conservatives, to act.

For Franz von Papen to facilitate the anti-Semitic fascists of Germany in the 1930s, he needed to assert—belief is a different issue—that there were no other options and the greater good was being facilitated. In 1932, when Papen seized control of the German state of Prussia—*Preußenschlag,* as the action is called in German—he insisted then and in his memoirs that he had no choice. Gregory Neilson writes in *Analysing Franz von Papen's Memoirs and His Role in the Nazi Rise to Power,*

Papen justified this action in his memoirs by claiming that the state was in imminent danger of being seized by the communists, "Schleicher told me of a report he had received from a senior official in the Prussian Ministry of the Interior. It seemed that negotiations had been going on between Abbegg, the Social Democrat State Secretary, and Casper, a Communist member of the Prussian State Parliament. An alliance between the two Marxist parties was by no means so unlikely, and if it came about, would present a most menacing situation . . . we decided that this must be prevented. . . ."

In reality this "threat" was Papen's pretext to seize control of the Prussian state and police and thus to consolidate the power of the central government, thus paving the way for a more authoritarian system in Germany.[10]

On September 5, 2016, an article appeared in the conservative *Claremont Review of Books* titled "The Flight 93 Election" under the pen name of Publius Decius Mus. The essay was a plea for conservatives who were reluctant to back Donald Trump to put their concerns aside because the alternative was so dangerous it posed an existential threat to the nation:

2016 is the Flight 93 election: charge the cockpit or you die. You may die anyway. You—or the leader of your party—may make it into the cockpit and not know how to fly or land the plane. There are no guarantees.

Except one: if you don't try, death is certain. To compound the metaphor: a Hillary Clinton presidency is Russian roulette with a semi-auto. With Trump, at least you can spin the cylinder and take your chances.[11]

The construct and presentation of the piece, from appearing in a scholarly journal to the use of the pseudonym Publius Decius Mus, the name of a Roman consul who sacrificed himself to win victory in the Battle of Vesuvius in 340 B.C., gave it an air of weighty seriousness and was treated as such by those eagerly looking for excuses to admit in public they supported Trump. For all its intellectual window dressing, the basic argument presented was a grad school version of the racism later celebrated in the neo-Nazis' march in Charlottesville to protest the removal of a Confederate statue. America was under attack from nonwhite heathens, the Barbarians at the Gate, who threaten the values of white America:

Most important, the ceaseless importation of Third World foreigners with no tradition of, taste for, or experience in liberty means that the electorate grows more left, more Democratic, less Republican, less republican, and less traditionally American with every cycle. As does, of course, the U.S. population, which only serves to reinforce the two other causes outlined above. This is the core reason why the Left, the Democrats, and the bipartisan junta (categories distinct but very much overlapping) think they are on the cusp of a permanent victory that will forever obviate the need to pretend to respect democratic and constitutional niceties. Because they are.[12]

This is a familiar racist plea, and it is not surprising that the author at the time chose to keep his identity secret. (As a general rule, if you are afraid to be associated with your opinion in public, it's probably time to rethink your opinion.) David Duke delivered the same message when he proclaimed in Charlottesville, "We are determined to take our country back. We are going to fulfill the promises of Donald Trump. That's what we believed in. That's why we voted for Donald Trump, because he said he's going to take our country back."[13] The voice in "The Flight 93 Election" echoes less a heroic Roman consul of 350 B.C. and more an 1861 secessionist in Mississippi who justified his actions in documents like "A Declaration of the Immediate Causes Which Induce and Justify the Secession of the State of Mississippi from the Federal Union": "There was no choice left us but submission to the mandates of abolition, or a dissolution of the Union, whose principles had been subverted to work out our ruin."[14]

In more turgid and pretentious language than the Mississippi Confederates, the author of "The Flight 93 Election" makes the same case that the choice is so bleak there is no choice:

The election of 2016 is a test—in my view, the final test—of whether there is any *virtù* left in what used to be the core of the American nation. If they cannot rouse themselves simply to vote for the first candidate in a generation who pledges to advance their interests, and to vote against the one who openly boasts that she will do the opposite (a million more Syrians, anyone?), then they are doomed. They may not deserve the fate that will befall them, but they will suffer it regardless.[15]

"The final test." This is the language used to recruit suicide bombers, not a rational discussion of political choices in a civil society. The reality that so many Republicans feel the need to justify their support of Trump with these apocalyptic constructs is a telling indication of their desperate contortions to prove that doing what they know is wrong is in pursuit of some higher good. The writer of "The Flight 93 Election" turned out to be not a heroic warrior like his pen name but a former speechwriter for Rudy Giuliani named Michael Anton, proving that both boss and staffer can compete side by side in the humiliation derby of the Trump era. In classic Donald Trump style, Anton was rewarded with a White House job. An early essay under the same self-glorifying pseudonym titled "Toward a Sensible, Coherent Trumpism"—like the need not to use one's own name in defense of an American presidential candidate, recognizing the need to admit that "Trumpism" is neither sensible nor coherent is likely more telling than the writer realizes—was full of the same foreboding fear of a nonwhite, non-Christian world that is the essence of Trump-ism: "Only an insane society, or one desperate to prove its fidelity to some chimerical 'virtue,' would have increased Muslim immigration after the September 11th attacks. Yet that is exactly what the United States did. Trump has, for

the first time, finally forced the questions: Why? and can we
stop now?" As always with the religious fearmongering of the
Trump era, it is instructive to replace "Muslim" with "Jewish"
to crack the code of the real sentiment behind the anger. In the
same essay, Anton writes,

> Yes, of course, not all Muslims are terrorists, blah, blah,
> blah, etc. Even so, what good has Muslim immigration
> done for the United States and the American people? If
> we truly needed more labor—a claim that is manifestly
> false—what made it necessary to import any of that
> labor from the Muslim world?[16]

It seems reasonable to assume the author is aware he is
dismissing one-fourth of the world's population with "blah,
blah, blah, etc." To Anton, any potential benefits of Muslims
would be for "more labor," a characterization that any German of the 1930s and 1940s would recognize as *Untermensch*.
Though Anton doesn't have a PhD, as did Joseph Goebbels,
he's well educated and earnestly seems to believe he is present-
ing an intellectual framework to support the weight of the
chanting Trump rallies. When the Trump era and the preced-
ing descent of the Republican Party into a legitimizing force
for white nationalism are studied, it seems inevitable that
the greatest weight of history will rest not with the Trump
voters or even the red-faced Trump rallyists screaming their
anger at the press, but with those like Anton and the leaders
of the Republican Party who failed a fundamental test of civic
decency. They broke a basic bond of trust that those handed

a role of power in a functioning democracy would treat the gift as both priceless and fragile, what Abraham Lincoln called "the legacy bequeathed to us."[17] Collectively, they are the indolent children of inherited wealth, removed by generations from those who last made the fortune—the Greatest Generation—and too self-absorbed and selfish to consider what they in turn might leave for the next generations. The assumption they make is that there will also be a civil society that respects differing opinions and rejects authoritarianism because they inherited it and assume it is a basic privilege that comes with their natural place in the world. The alternative, responsible role is outlined in *How Democracies Die:*

> Successful gatekeeping requires that mainstream parties isolate and defeat extremist forces, a behavior political scientist Nancy Bermeo calls "distancing." Prodemocratic parties may engage in distancing in several ways. First, they can keep would-be authoritarians off party ballots at election time. This requires that they resist the temptation to nominate these extremists for higher office even when they can potentially deliver votes.
>
> Second, parties can root out extremists in the grass roots of their own ranks. . . .
>
> Third, prodemocratic parties can avoid all alliances with antidemocratic parties and candidates. . . .
>
> Fourth, prodemocratic parties can act to systematically isolate, rather than legitimize, extremists. This requires that politicians avoid acts—such as German Conservatives' joint rallies with Hitler in the early 1930s

or Caldera's speech sympathizing with Chávez—that help to "normalize" or provide public respectability to authoritarian figures.

Finally, whenever extremists emerge as serious electoral contenders, mainstream parties must forge a united front to defeat them. . . . [I]n extraordinary times, courageous party leadership means putting democracy and country before party and articulating to voters what is at stake.[18]

Like the inability to imagine Donald Trump winning, there is a great failure of imagination to contemplate the damage done to American civil society by Trump's presidency and the degradation of any moral authority of a center-right party. Shortly before the 2016 election, when the consensus was that Trump was going to lose and lose badly, the RNC chairman, Reince Priebus, told a political operative friend, "As soon as this election is over, we're going to just bury it in the backyard and act like it never happened." Now many in what passes for the Republican establishment view the Trump presidency the same way. Yes, a white nationalist who ran on a Muslim ban and calls Mexicans rapists, a man who has no sense of truth and little of right and wrong, a man who wrote hush-money checks for a porn star in the Oval Office is president, but, hey, we cut marginal tax rates for corporations. Republicans have become the alcoholics at the bar who promise themselves they can quit drinking whenever they so desire. But let me finish this drink first. In *How Democracies Die,* the authors described a set of four behavioral warning signs that can help us know an authoritarian when we see one. We should worry when a politician 1) rejects, in words or action, the democratic rules of the game, 2) denies the legitimacy of opponents, 3) tolerates or encourages violence, or 4) indicates a willingness to curtail the civil liberties of opponents, including the media.[19]

Republicans in the Donald Trump era are guilty of all four. A review:

1. *Rejects, in words or action, the democratic rules of the game.* Like much of civil society, American democracy functions under a combination of specific laws and assumed norms. As the Mueller Report makes clear, Trump would likely be indicted for obstruction of justice, were he not a sitting president. He has used the White House as a corporate branding tool for his personal gain; is the first president in modern history to refuse to release his tax returns (after promising repeatedly to do so); praised a congressman for assaulting a reporter; attacked the foundations of the American criminal justice system at its highest levels with attacks on the Justice Department, FBI, and CIA; and encourages staffers to break laws both large and small, from refusing to respond to congressional subpoenas to ignoring the Hatch Act. He's refused to allow records of his meetings with foreign leaders hostile to the United States, like Vladimir Putin. Hundreds of thousands of dollars of taxpayer funds are spent at his golf clubs, hotels, and restaurants. His company charges the Secret Service for the golf carts they rent (at exorbitant fees) to follow him in

security details. Like no president in U.S. history, Trump has taken the presidency, built in a profit margin, and charged the American public. He has refused to acknowledge the overwhelming evidence of the largest attack by a hostile foreign power on the American election system in U.S. history. He has openly discussed not leaving office when constitutionally required. Trump has demanded the attorney general of the United States act as his personal attorney, putting his interest first, the way Roy Cohn did when he worked for Trump. All of these insults and attacks on American democracy have been either cheered by Republicans or, at best, ignored. Those who refuse to specifically support various acts of outrage by Trump more often than not simply shrug and pretend not to be aware. When Trump has left, it is safe to say the ranks of the "Good Republicans" who maintain they really didn't know the extent of what Trump did will make Washington feel a lot like 1946 Berlin.

2. Denies the legitimacy of opponents. Trump launched his campaign for president with an attack on the legitimacy of the U.S. president. By challenging Barack Obama's birth certificate, he was challenging the legality of the presidency and accusing the U.S. government of being illegal. Like so many of his actions to come, the Trump attack was meant to undermine democracy itself and to establish himself as the arbiter of what was legal and illegal. Just as Trump would later rant, "I alone can fix it," the accusation that Obama was foreign born and therefore illegal was predicated on secret information that only he held. This theme of "secret information" would be a thread throughout the Trump presidency, from

assurances he received from Kim Jong Un on nuclear weapons
to a trade deal with the Mexican government. Anticipating
defeat in 2016, Trump crossed the country denouncing a
rigged election manipulated by dark forces that included the
press. "The election is being rigged by corrupt media pushing
completely false allegations and outright lies," he accused,
usually combined with his now standard charge that Hillary
Clinton was a criminal. "Hillary Clinton should have been
prosecuted and should be in jail. Instead she is running for
president in what looks like a rigged election."[20] Trump led
the party that once defined itself as the "law and order" party
into Nuremberg-rally-like chants of "Lock her up."

   3. *Tolerates or encourages violence.* Trump, who went to
great lengths to avoid serving in the military, where he might
encounter actual violence, gleefully urges his supporters at
rallies to "beat the crap out of" protesters, just "knock the
hell . . . I promise you I will pay for the legal fees. I promise, I promise." He's praised a congressman who attacked
a reporter, saying, "Any guy who can do a body slam, he is
my type!" In a speech in front of law enforcement officers,
Trump urged them to get "rough" on gang members.[21] When
the *Morning Joe* host Joe Scarborough asked Trump in 2015
about Vladimir Putin's record of killing journalists, Trump
answered, "Well, I think that our country does plenty of killing, too, Joe."[22] Trump has lamented that other Republicans
aren't "tough enough." In an interview with Breitbart in
March 2019, Trump said, "You know, the left plays a tougher
game. It's very funny. I actually think that the people on
the right are tougher, but they don't play it tougher. O.K.? I

can tell you I have the support of the police, the support of the military, the support of the Bikers for Trump. I have the tough people, but they don't play it tough—until they go to a certain point, and then it would be very bad, very bad."[23] At a rally before the 2018 midterm elections, when a protester was removed, Trump reacted, "You see these little arms, these little arms? . . . Where are the Bikers for Trump? Where are the police? Where are the military? Where are—ICE? Where are the border patrol?" As Jonathan Chait wrote for *New York* magazine, "Trump isn't inciting violence by mistake, but on purpose. He just told us."[24]

4. Indicates a willingness to curtail the civil liberties of opponents, including the media. Trump has launched an assault on the First Amendment unlike any president in history, threatening to use the power of the government to attack media he dislikes, from *The Washington Post* to CNN, as "the enemy of the people." His knowledge of the Bill of Rights is limited to a passing knowledge of the Second Amendment, and he has spent his presidency attacking the judicial process that is the essence of American civil liberties. The Constitution means as much to Donald Trump as the rules of golf, a game at which he routinely cheats.

The assumption that the post-Trump American political system will revert to standards of normalcy that existed before Trump is yet another excuse Republicans use to justify their support of him. It's why Republicans are so desperate to assert that Trump has supported policy that any Republican president would have supported. This is like going to a wedding in which a gunfight breaks out between the groom and the bride's family after vows are exchanged and dismissing the fatalities because the ceremony had been legally performed: "What counts is they were married, never mind the bodies in the church." This is a view of government as nothing more than the sum total of bills passed or judges appointed, as if it were possible to assemble a human being from a collection of body parts. It completely ignores the true essence of a civil society that reflects the collective values and aspirations of a diverse country. In the Trump years, Republicans have sent a message that lying is useful and productive, racism is acceptable, the press is the enemy, and a strong-man authoritarian head of government is the ideal.

It's unfair to blame Trump for how Republican elected officials have responded to his candidacy and election. Each had a choice, and in overwhelming numbers these officials made a personal choice to support a man each knew was wildly unqualified to be president. It's a familiar pattern, and every Republican can wish upon an American exceptionalism star and it means nothing.

Some version of this story has repeated itself throughout the world over the last century, with a cast of political outsiders, including Adolf Hitler:

> Getúlio Vargas in Brazil, Alberto Fujimori in Peru, and Hugo Chávez in Venezuela, came to power on the same path: from the inside, via elections or alliances with powerful political figures. In each instance, elites believed the invitation to power would *contain* the outsider, leading to a restoration of control by mainstream politicians.

But their plans backfired. A lethal mix of ambition, fear, and miscalculation conspired to lead them to the same fateful mistake: willingly handing over the keys of power to an autocrat-in-the-making.[25]

For me, much of this is personal. I helped elect so many who now support Donald Trump, and I know, because I know these men and women well, that they find Trump repulsive and a degradation of their life's work and espoused values. And yet they support him, knowing on some level that it is damaging to every civic value they have previously held. There is a mutually self-reinforcing abandonment of any sense of higher duty than serving the political moment. It is a contagious failure of responsibility masked under whatever ludicrous cover story the Republican Party is pushing at the moment.

For decades, Republicans fought the culture wars because they believed that culture defined a society. Now they wake up every morning and rush to compete in the embarrassment derby that is their daily fare, striving to find new ways to defend the indefensible. Few are naive enough to really believe what they say, but the palace of lies is a comfortable mansion with many rooms. They lash out whenever one of their own tells the truth, like Justin Amash, because the simple power of honesty melts their world like ice on a hot stove. They tell themselves that the alternative is unacceptable: that if they don't support and encourage a man who assaults women and lies instinctively, they will soon find themselves facing the red armies of socialism and the country will start to look like . . .

Sweden. There is nothing new or particularly interesting about this deceit. Republicans are linked to a vast life-support system of lies, terrified that the truth will unplug the machine.

American history has never seen a party so unified in perpetuating a massive fraud. This isn't the action of a rogue president like Watergate but a deliberate, calculated decision for a major governing party of the most powerful nation in the history of the world to join hands and deny what they know is true: that Donald Trump is a threat to the country. At its root is an acceptance of a betrayal of their country that they try to disguise by suppressing those in their ranks who put their country over their party. These people don't hate America, but they are weak men and women who decided long ago their self-worth was determined by winning elections. One of their favorite refrains off the record to reporters is that it would have been much worse had they not intervened. What will the lasting impact be of their collective failure? No one knows, of course, but I suspect they are knowingly or unknowingly destroying the value of center-right government for generations to come. And that would be under the best-case circumstances. This was their moment to stand for something, and they chose to stand for reelection. Let us remember.

8

THE EMPIRE'S
LAST STAND

It's not the voting that's democracy, it's the counting.
—Tom Stoppard, *Jumpers*

The Republican Party, like the Democratic Party, is a vastly wealthy, powerful force. Though there is no mention of parties in the Constitution, these conglomerates have come to be the most powerful forces in our democracy. Each party is a multibillion-dollar industry that, like any powerful business, will respond when threatened. The greater the threat, the more desperate the reaction. Though no one inside the Republican Party likes to admit it, a deep fear lurks in the heart of the party: a fear of the future. The Trump obsession with immigrants from Mexico and Central America is motivated by his own racism, but it also reflects the knowledge that every new nonwhite voter in America is a threat to the existence of the Republican Party. How rapidly is America changing? Here's a snapshot of the 2020 electorate from the Pew Research Center:

> In raw numbers, a projected 32 million Hispanics will be eligible to vote in 2020, compared with 30 million blacks.

The population of Asians eligible to vote will reach an estimated 11 million in 2020, which is more than double the 5 million who were eligible to vote in 2000, accounting for 5% of next year's electorate.

Taken together, this strong growth among minority populations means that a third of eligible voters will be nonwhite in 2020, up from about a quarter in 2000. This increase is at least partially linked to immigration and naturalization patterns: One-in-ten eligible voters in the 2020 election will have been born outside the U.S., the highest share since at least 1970.[1]

If the Pew projections prove accurate, this will mean that the white vote has declined from 77 percent in 2004 to 68 percent in 2020. That's a huge decrease. And when coupled with the drop in Hispanic support for Bush of just over 40 percent in 2004 to Trump's likely target of between 25 percent and 30 percent in 2020, it's, well, problematic for Trump and all Republicans. I still believe Trump should be favored in 2020 due largely to his overwhelming financial advantage now that federal funding for presidential campaigns has ended, but the demographic hill will be harder to climb. Looking ahead, in a joint project with the Center for American Progress, American Enterprise Institute, and Brookings Institution, simulations were run of future elections from 2020 to 2036 based on likely demographic trends and past history of performance by each party. Their model runs three different scenarios, from most favorable to each party to least favorable. Each has Republicans losing the Electoral College from 2024 to 2036.[2]

These trends have been evident for over two decades, and as someone who has sat in the room for five presidential campaigns and tried to figure out how to get a Republican candidate over the 270 mark, the math has been increasingly oppressive. The obvious choice for the party was to expand its appeal beyond white voters. That diagnosis was as obvious as telling a patient with lung cancer to quit smoking. But at the same time, Republicans were taking steps to change the electoral math by making it harder for nonwhites to vote. In this, they were continuing a long tradition of efforts by powerful white politicians to remain in power by suppressing votes.

Today a group of oddball conservatives such as the former convicted felon Dinesh D'Souza—pardoned by Trump—go to elaborate efforts to defend the Republican Party by pointing to the segregationist history of southern Democrats.[3] For decades during the Jim Crow era, there was no functioning Republican Party in the South, and, yes, segregationists like Mississippi's senator James Eastland were Democrats.[4] But to focus on their party label is to miss the point. Whether they had a D or an R by their name meant less than having a big W by their name, W for "white." The white power structure has a long history of making it more difficult for blacks to vote, from poll taxes to literacy tests to violence. My home state of Mississippi developed what became the blueprint of efforts to exclude black voters with the 1875 Mississippi Plan. It was an effort by whites to reclaim power lost after Reconstruction, when blacks were allowed to vote for the first time. A new state constitution was adopted in 1890 that required payment of a poll tax and the ability to read and interpret any section of the Mississippi State Constitution. There was little pretext of the broad intent of the new constitution; it made interracial marriage illegal and mandated separate schools for blacks and whites.[5] Similar laws were soon adopted in other southern states.

Barry Goldwater's opposition to the Civil Rights Act, which made Jim Crow voter-suppression laws illegal, was the defining moment for the modern Republican Party. That year 93 percent of blacks voted for Lyndon Johnson, and the die was cast that has led the Republican Party to evolve into the predominantly white party it is today.[6] As the percentage of the white electorate steadily declined, the Republican Party faced an existential choice. Was it possible to change such that it could attract more nonwhite voters, or would it go down the road of using every means possible to fight the demographic trend of declining white voters by making it more difficult for nonwhite voters, particularly black voters, to participate in the election? This was a fundamental battle for the soul of the Republican Party. In July 2005, the RNC chairman, Ken Mehlman, with whom I had worked closely in the 2000 Bush campaign, went before the NAACP national convention and offered an apology for past Republican efforts to use race as a wedge issue with white voters: "Some Republicans gave up on winning the African American vote, looking the other way or trying to benefit politically from racial polarization. I am here today as the Republican Chairman to tell you we were wrong."[7] As was noted in news coverage, Mehlman was referencing the so-called southern strategy adopted by Nixon. The Pat Buchanan–Kevin Phillips memo to President Nixon referenced in chapter 1 is the original document of what became the very successful efforts by Republicans to convert white Democratic voters in the South into Republicans.

But Ken Mehlman's was a lonely and largely ignored voice in the Republican Party. Among some of us who worked in the 2000 Bush campaign, there is something of a wistful parlor game wondering what a Bush administration might have been like, absent 9/11. His first major legislation was the education reform bill No Child Left Behind, which he signed with Senator Ted Kennedy looking over his shoulder. But that's a world that doesn't exist, and any chance for transformation of the Republican Party into the big tent it then espoused to be has been lost. While the RNC went through its exercise of analyzing the party's problems after its 2012 loss and made the obvious conclusion that in a country that was becoming less white, the Republican Party needed to become less white, Republicans across the country were also quietly but effectively taking steps to balance the electoral equation by suppressing nonwhite votes. It paid off. For the first time in twenty years, African American votes declined in 2016, with turnout dropping 7 percent from 2012.[8]

By analyzing specific states where Republicans passed new voting laws, one can track the cause and effect of voter-suppression efforts. None of these laws blatantly admitted their true purpose—the country is not Mississippi in 1875—but it is disingenuous for Republicans to claim they did not know exactly what they were doing. Wisconsin is a state that Donald Trump won by 22,748 votes out of almost 3 million votes cast. In 2011, under Governor Scott Walker, the state passed a strict voter-ID law that U.S. district courts blocked. The premise for voter-ID requirements is to fight voter fraud, but those of us who work in elections know what the court concluded: there is almost no voter fraud in American elections. In his decision, Judge Lynn Adelman wrote, "The evidence at trial established that virtually no voter impersonation occurs in Wisconsin. The defendants could not point to a single instance of known voter impersonation occurring in Wisconsin at any time in the recent past."[9] The ruling was challenged and a ferocious legal battle ensued, reaching the Supreme Court. Weeks before the November 2016 election, a judge for the U.S. District Court for the Eastern District of Wisconsin allowed the state to apply the voter-ID requirement. It is impossible to quantify exactly the number of voters who were discouraged from voting by the new law. But as Carol Anderson in her analysis of voter restrictions, *One Person, No Vote,* described it,

> In Wisconsin, for example, black voting rates plummeted from a high of 78 percent in 2012 to less than 50 percent in 2016. In Milwaukee County, which is overwhelmingly African American, fifty thousand fewer votes were cast in a state that Donald Trump won by only twenty-seven thousand ballots.[10]

After he won on November 8, 2016, Donald Trump became the first winner of a presidential race to attack the legitimacy of his own victory. Weeks after the election, Trump tweeted, "In addition to winning the Electoral College in a landslide, I won the popular vote if you deduct the millions of people who voted illegally."[11] It's easy to dismiss this as another boastful lie from a pathological liar, like his claim on 9/11 that he now owned the tallest building in New York. But it's much more. Trump doesn't seem to realize that if millions of voters were actually illegal, it would invalidate his election, because it would be impossible to know for whom they cast votes. In Trump's mind—and it sadly reflects the minds of many Republicans—the assumption is that any illegal voters would be Democratic voters with the associated assumption that they must be illegal Hispanic voters. As a way of trying to justify voter-suppression steps, the Republican Party has invested heavily in the myth of voter fraud. The fraud is trying to convince the public there is voter fraud of any significance. I've worked in campaigns since 1978, and I don't know of a single race in which illegal voters were remotely a factor. Does some illegal voting happen? Sure, just as elephantiasis does occur in America. But should elephantiasis be the focus of the National Institutes of Health instead of cancer? Probably not.

None of the various voter-suppression tools employed by Republicans are overtly race based, if for no other reason than they would be illegal. But discrimination is a bad look—or at least it has been since the civil rights days. Before Donald Trump, I and many of my Republican consulting colleagues would have thought that any embrace of racism would alienate moderate Republicans. But those of us who made that assumption seem to have been wrong. The ability to rationalize the overt bigotry of "good people on both sides" has proven shockingly common among Republicans, who still support Donald Trump at more than 90 percent. But voter suppression doesn't need to rely on race-based formulas to work. The modern political calculation of suppressing non-Republican voters is not complicated. Those at the lower end

of the economic spectrum are less likely to vote Republican.
And those same people are less likely to have access to the
basic tools of the middle class that most of us take for
granted—like easy access to a polling place or government-
issued ID. Implementing stringent voter-ID laws and reducing
the number of polling places and/or reducing early-voter and
vote-by-mail options disproportionately target voters who
are less likely to be Republicans. Carol Anderson describes it
accurately in *One Person, No Vote:*

> The devices the Republicans used are variations on a
> theme going back more than 150 years. They target the
> socioeconomic characteristics of a people (poverty, lack
> of mobility, illiteracy, etc.) and then soak the new laws
> in "racially neutral justifications—such as administra-
> tive efficiency" or "fiscal responsibility"—to cover the
> discriminatory intent. Republican lawmakers then act
> aggrieved, shocked, and wounded that anyone would
> question their stated purpose for excluding millions of
> American citizens from the ballot box.[12]

In *The Politics of Voter Suppression,* Tova Wang draws a
similar conclusion:

> Until the second half of the twentieth century, the
> Democrats were the main culprits. Over the past fifty
> years, however, Republicans have most frequently and
> deftly employed election law and procedures to help
> their party win elections. As the country remains ideo-
> logically divided, and outcomes of local, some statewide,

and presidential elections have the potential to be close, contemporary Republicans have made it a central part of their election strategy to enact laws and call for practices that will reduce turnout among those who tend to vote Democratic, at least at the margins—where elections can often be won or lost.[13]

It's difficult for me to express how much it pains me that Anderson's and Wang's descriptions are exactly correct. Given the overwhelmingly white composition of the Republican Party, the efforts to make it more difficult to vote reflect much of the same instinct as the Jim Crow–era laws. Ari Berman described the impact of a poll tax in Alabama. The law was not specifically targeting black voters, but the impact was profound:

> "When you pay $1.50 for a poll tax, in Dallas County, I believe you disenfranchise 10 Negroes," Henry Fontaine Reese, a delegate from Selma, argued at Alabama's Constitutional Convention of 1901. "Give us this $1.50 for educational purposes and for the disenfranchisement of a vicious and useless class." Reese represented what Ralph McGill of the *Atlanta Constitution* called "Black Belt thinking," which infected not only Selma but so much of the South. After adoption of the 1901 constitution, the number of black registered votes in Alabama fell from 182,000 to 4,000.[14]

It took the Twenty-Fourth Amendment to the Constitution in 1964 to abolish the poll tax:

The right of citizens of the United States to vote in any primary or other election for President or Vice President, for electors for President or Vice President, or for Senator or Representative in Congress, shall not be denied or abridged by the United States or any State by reason of failure to pay poll tax or other tax.

But as I write this in the autumn of 2019, a coalition of civil rights groups is suing the State of Florida for passing legislation signed by the Republican governor that the suit claims is an attempt to institute a new poll tax. And they are right. The new legislation follows a 2018 amendment to the Florida Constitution that granted voting rights to the estimated 1.4 million Floridians with a prior felony conviction. The follow-up legislation requires those who had been convicted of a felony to pay all court fees and fines that are outstanding before they are allowed to vote. The intent of this is no different from that of the Alabama Constitution of 1901, charging voters $1.50 to vote. What percentages of those former felons are black? "In 2016, more than 418,000 black people out of a black voting-age population of more than 2.3 million, or 17.9 percent of potential black voters in Florida, had finished sentences but couldn't vote due to a felony record, according to the Sentencing Project," *Vox* wrote shortly after the 2018 amendment was passed granting voting rights to former felons.[15]

Along with poll taxes, so-called literacy tests were standards in the Jim Crow era. Before the Voting Rights Act, Louisiana had this test. It was intended to be given to anyone who could not prove he or she graduated from the fifth grade, but in practice the local polling-place officials could demand anyone take it. (Who has a copy of their grade school transcript to prove they had graduated from the fifth grade?)[16]

It had to be completed in ten minutes, and one mistake disqualified a voter. The new voter suppression of the Republican Party is almost an inevitable outcome of the party's failure to expand beyond white voters, combined with a self-rationalizing conviction that winning by any means is more than justified; it is required to save the country from . . . something. Socialism is the current "Greater Threat" that is being trotted out on the field. But on the sidelines are other "Greater Threats" resting for a return. The key player of recent years has been the Muslim "Greater Threat." Republican legislators have introduced more than two hundred anti-Sharia bills across the country. The Republican Party was perfectly happy to support a nominee for president running on a "total and complete ban of Muslims entering the United States" platform.

But the looming threat of some socialist takeover of America or Sharia law becoming the new Supreme Court standard is all nonsense. And most Republican elected officials know it's nonsense, just as they know Donald Trump is an unqualified idiot. But what many Republican politicians actually do believe is that they represent the "real" America, and they are somewhere from uncomfortable to frightened by America's changing landscape. Instead of embracing the change that renews America and defines America, Republicans have more often than not reacted like the white neighborhood that feared property values would drop once the "wrong" kinds of people moved in. You see this in the very language used by Republicans: "working-class voters" usually means white working-class voters. "Ordinary Americans" means non-urban Christians, mostly white. It is reminiscent of when Mississippi's governor Ross Barnett addressed a Jewish group in Jackson, Mississippi, with "We are all good Christian men and women." The common thread is fear. Fear of change, fear of the unknown, fear of losing power while forgetting the purpose of power.

Fear is at the heart of most conspiracy theories, and the current Republican Party is driven by conspiracy theories, a result of years of nutty radio mixed with nutty internet supercharged by a nutty president. When they are the stuff of midnight radio shows, wildly elaborate conspiracy theories have a certain amusingly harmless quality, but when they are driven by a president and accepted by his political party, conspiracies are a serious attack on the connective tissues of trust that hold a civil society together. When a president claims—and repeats over and over—that millions voted illegally and the entire apparatus of his party accepts this as true by silence, if not by active confirmation, it can be used to justify extreme measures that further the political goals of the party. Of course it makes sense to demand IDs at polling places when millions are voting illegally. Of course it makes sense to spend billions to build a wall on our southern border when America is being invaded with illegals who come here to rape, murder, . . . and vote. This, of course, is an insane notion. Illegal voting has long been a felony, and the idea that of all the felonies possible to commit, someone would risk the consequences of a felony conviction to vote is one of the more almost-charming absurdities imaginable. Our problem in America is getting people to vote, not stopping illegals.

Conspiracies are a key element of the Trump Republican effort to build an alternative universe in which their lies will be truth. When you insist that the sky is green, the best argument is not to deny the sky is blue but to build a world in which the sky is in fact green. Then everyone who says it is blue is clearly a liar. Like so much about Donald Trump's relationship to the Republican Party, he merely represents the next step in a process that has been half a century in the making. Trump's Deep State is just a variation of Joe McCarthy's mythical Communists infesting the State Department, the "enemies within." The two had the same lawyer, Roy Cohn. The difference between Joe McCarthy and Donald Trump is that in the 1950s there were those in the Republican Party who would stand up to McCarthy, while now there are few with the integrity to confront Donald Trump. In the 1950s, America had a president, Dwight Eisenhower, who saw the danger of Joe McCarthy. In the second decade of the twenty-first century, Joe McCarthy *is* president.

Labeling any media you don't like as "fake news" is an all-encompassing conspiracy theory that makes truth an enemy. Same goes with denouncing anyone in government who might stand in the way of an authoritarian president as a member of the shadowy "Deep State." The Trump/right-wing conspiracies have a common thread of labeling truth a conspiracy. It's reflective of the general projection that characterizes Trump and is becoming increasingly common in Republican politics:

Trump is a racist who elevated white nationalists like Steve Bannon from lurking in the shadows of society to the White House. Trump's defense is to attack others on race. "Hillary Clinton is a bigot who sees people of color only as votes, not as human beings worthy of a better future," he said in the 2016 campaign.[17] As *Psychology Today* wrote, "Too often, Trump sounds like he is turning things inside (of him) out, engaging in the unconscious defense mechanism that Freud called projection: the attribution of one's own forbidden— and typically malevolent—motives, impulses, or emotions to others."[18]

Republicans are increasingly uneasy in a world of change. That uniquely American sense of optimism that was once claimed by both Democrats and Republicans has been replaced with a dark foreboding of what lies ahead for a threatened America. No longer is to be born in America to win life's lottery and know you are among the luckiest on earth; in the Trump Republican view, Americans are suckers, victims, the mark for a hostile world. Everyone is out to get America, from the Canadians to the Chinese. Anger has replaced gratitude. In a view of the world that has America under siege, extreme measures are needed, and good men and women must do what it takes to defend America. This means electing Republicans, and how you elect them is of less importance than the necessity of winning. The voter suppression that is increasingly embraced by a Republican Party unburdened by a watchful Voting Rights Act is not a subversion of democracy but a defense of democracy. To these Republicans, burning the village to save it makes perfect sense.

Carol Anderson, in *One Person, No Vote,* sums up the intent and result of the Republican efforts to change the makeup of the electorate in the 2016 election, in which the African American vote declined for the first time in twenty years:

> Minority voters did not just refuse to show up; Republican legislatures and governors systematically blocked African Americans, Hispanics, and Asian Americans from the polls. Pushed by both the impending demographic collapse of the Republican Party, whose overwhelmingly white constituency is becoming an ever smaller share of the electorate, and the GOP's extremist inability to craft policies that speak to an increasingly diverse nation, the Republicans opted to disfranchise rather than reform. The GOP, therefore, enacted a range of undemocratic and desperate measures to block the access of African American, Latino, and other minority voters to the ballot box. Using a series of voter suppression tactics, the GOP harassed, obstructed, frustrated, and purged American citizens from having a say in their own democracy.[19]

The Republican Party will signal that it is a healthy, growing political party when it embraces efforts to make it easier to register and vote for all segments of the electorate, not just Republicans and likely Republicans. What does it say about a party that it opposes automatically registering every voter at age eighteen or opposes efforts to register voters automatically when they receive or renew a driver's license? The country has a crisis of voter participation: half of the eligible voters do not register, and of those who do, only half actually vote. In a *Washington Post* article headlined "New Data Makes It Clear: Nonvoters Handed Trump the Presidency," Philip Bump analyzes a study by the Pew Research Center that reveals that "those who didn't vote are as responsible for the outcome of the election as those who did." Bump writes,

> As we noted shortly after the election, about 30 percent of Americans were eligible to vote but decided not to, a higher percentage than the portion of the country who voted for either Trump or his Democratic opponent, Hillary Clinton. Pew's data shows that almost half of the nonvoters were nonwhite and two-thirds were under age 50. More than half of those who didn't vote earned less than $30,000 a year; more than half of those who did vote were over age 50.
>
> Demographic groups that preferred Trump were three times as likely to be a bigger part of the voter pool than nonvoters. Among groups that preferred Clinton, they were about 50 percent more likely to be a bigger part of the nonvoting community.[20]

Nonvoters were disproportionately poorer, nonwhite, and younger, all groups that, if they had voted, favored Hillary Clinton over Donald Trump by wide margins. Republicans put up a smoke screen of reasons to try to explain why they are against efforts to encourage voting by automatic registration, which, at base level, is a fundamentally antidemocratic instinct. When Oregon passed legislation to register any resident who has contact with the DMV retroactively to 2013, every Republican legislator opposed it. The Republican state party chair, Suzanne Gallagher, said,

> We do not support government automatically registering every Oregonian to vote, as these Amendments would require. This should be the choice of the citizen, not the mandate of the State. This is one more difference between the two parties. Democrats believe the government should register people to vote. Republicans believe people have an individual responsibility to vote.[21]

Gallagher cited concerns of privacy because being registered to vote places your name and address on a voting roll list, which is a public document. It's an argument that in itself has the whiff of conspiracy floating over it, a fear of some unknown forces that might take advantage of . . . a voter roll. It would stand to reason that for this to be legitimate, some negative consequences must have befallen those who had registered. But that's applying logic to a problem no one really believes is a problem. The same people who have no problem mandating reproductive choices for women cite personal freedom as an opposition to registering voters. Nonsense. Republicans in Oregon don't want to make it easier for those who are less likely to vote for Republicans to participate in the system.

Of course another reaction might be to analyze why it is the Republican Party is less appealing to those who are poorer, younger, and nonwhite and try to change the party so that it has more appeal, rather than trying to block these groups from voting. But Republicans have thrown their power behind making sure more of "their" people vote instead of trying to make the party more appealing. It's a losing strategy in a country that is changing as rapidly as America. Republicans have fallen in love with the Electoral College because they see it as a way for the "real America" to balance the power of the "coastal elites." Only once since 1988 have Republicans won the popular vote in a presidential race. A sane reaction to that reality would be to acknowledge that the party must fundamentally change. Instead, the reaction is a fierce defense of the Electoral College, which has allowed two Republicans, George W. Bush and Donald Trump, to become president with the minority of the vote. I worked in the Bush campaign, and some of us would darkly joke, "Anybody can become president when you get more votes. To lose by half a million and become president takes professionals." It seemed funny at the time. Less so now.

It has become a fundamental tenet of the modern Republican Party to hate California, which is extraordinarily revealing. Something is deeply disturbed about a political party if it considers the most populous state part of the long list of "otherness" that Republicans see as separating the true America from something dangerous and anti-American. How did this happen? How did the state that gave us Ronald Reagan, the state that defined for the world what it was to be an American, the state with the largest number of military bases and the greatest farms of America, the state that built the world's first great post-automobile city, the state with the industries that changed the world, from Apple to Hollywood—how did that become for Republicans an alien place to be scorned and ridiculed? As Michael Grunwald wrote in a piece for *Politico* called "Trump's War on California," California is thriving by any measure, but

> that hasn't stopped Republicans from making California their go-to nightmare scenario. In 2018, Senator Ted Cruz warned that liberals wanted Texas to be "just like California, right down to the tofu and silicone and dyed hair." Democratic candidates for governor were accused of trying to turn Nevada and Florida into California, and Colorado into "RadiCalifornia." In the Georgia governor's race, Republican Brian Kemp's stump-speech mantra about Democrat Stacey Abrams was that she was trying to import "radical California values." The Republican National Committee's nickname for Harris in its news releases is "California Kamala," and it rarely mentions her without mentioning her "San Francisco values."[22]

With the exception of the 1964 Goldwater landslide, Republicans carried California in every post–World War II presidential election until 1988. Then it started to slip away for Republicans. Now the Republican Party is officially the third-largest group of voters, behind Democrats and independents, which in California are called NPP (no party preference) voters. Donald Trump barely broke 30 percent in 2016. One out of every eleven voters in the country lives in California, and there is a long history of trends in California as harbingers of what America will become. As the largest state, it has often served to be an insight into what the country is becoming, and it should terrify Republicans. In 1980, California was 66 percent white and 19 percent Hispanic.[23] In the 2010 census, it was 40 percent white and 37 percent Hispanic.[24] This gets to the heart of why Republicans have now decided they hate California. Not surprisingly, California has decided it hates Republicans: There are a lot of brown people in California. A lot.

In 1994, Governor Pete Wilson ran a now-infamous ad in his reelection campaign for governor that showed a video of Mexicans climbing over a border wall with an ominous voice-over: "They keep coming. Two million illegal immigrants in California. The federal government won't stop them at the border, yet requires us to pay billions to take care of them."[25] That same year a statewide initiative, Proposition 187, was on the ballot. Marketed under the "SOS: Save Our State" label, it called for the termination of all government benefits, from education to health care, for illegal immigrants. It passed with almost 60 percent of the vote, but with only 31 percent of Hispanic support.[26] Pete Wilson won reelection, but the measure sent a signal to Hispanic legal residents of California that they were unwanted by Republicans. The parallels to Donald Trump's announcing his campaign calling Mexicans "rapists" are obvious. By contrast, in 1994 in Texas, George W. Bush ran for governor with a welcoming message to Mexican Americans, and it helped secure the Republican Party's dominance in Texas. In his 1998 reelection, George W. Bush had almost 50 percent of the Hispanic vote. As *The New York Times* reported in an article analyzing Bush's direct appeal to Hispanic voters, "When Mr. Bush was re-elected by a landslide, he also by one estimate won nearly half the Hispanic vote statewide. He even won El Paso. It seemed like political magic; he had found votes in places Republicans usually dared not tread."[27]

In the 2018 Senate race, that support dropped to 35 percent for Ted Cruz, a number still above the sub-30 percent both Mitt Romney and Donald Trump received. But it's a warning sign for Republicans as Texas becomes increasingly Hispanic. What sort of future is there for the Republican Party? Good question.

9

HOW DO LIES END?

Watching the Republican Party is like watching a friend drink himself to death. There's a mix of sadness and anger tinged by a bit of sympathy for the misery he tries to hide. But alcoholism is a disease, and political cowardice is just what it looks like: weakness and opportunism mixed with fear and self-loathing. Most Republican elected officials wish that one of the other fifteen candidates who ran for president in 2016 were now in the White House. They love to whisper this to each other and to journalists off the record, as if this somehow absolves them of any responsibility for supporting a man who violates nearly every value they avowed their entire careers. Few realize this only makes them look even more pathetic and compromised.

Those who opposed Trump in 2016 but now accept him have evolved ever more fanciful rationalizations for their moral collapse, such as this piece in the *National Review:* "Acknowledge Trump's achievements and help him win reelection. Then roll out a new party, not as a spoiler but as support for conservative principles."[1] This from the magazine that famously ran an entire issue in February 2016 dedicated to the urgency of Republicans' defeating Trump. The issue was a collection of essays by various conservatives representing the spectrum of issues that have most defined modern conservatism, from cultural to foreign policy, arguing the urgency of defeating Donald Trump. Some of those authors—Mona Charen, a longtime conservative columnist, Dr. Russell Moore, a prominent Southern Baptist leader, and Bill Kristol, former editor of *The Weekly Standard*—have continued to stand by their principles and taken the associated heat. At the yearly gathering of conservatives known as CPAC, a security detail had to protect Mona Charen after she said it was wrong for conservatives to support the accused child molester Roy Moore or ignore the women who have accused Donald Trump. "You cannot claim that you stand for women and put up with that," she said.[2] The ex-governor of Arkansas Mike Huckabee, a former Southern Baptist preacher, called for Russell Moore to be fired by the Southern Baptist church for Moore's principled stand on Trump. Huckabee said he was "utterly stunned that Russell Moore is being paid by Southern Baptists to insult" Trump.[3] With little room in the conservative media for anything but lavish praise of Trump, Bill Kristol's *Weekly Standard* went out of business.[4]

As I write this in the fall of 2019, the 2020 election looms large with an impossible-to-predict outcome. As discussed before, since the demise of federal funding for presidential general elections, an incumbent president has a tremendous financial advantage. But if Trump wins or loses, it is a fantasy to think that the impact of a nation's major center-right party embracing a racist unprepared to be president with Trump's deep psychological problems will not be lasting. Perhaps what passes for the establishment in the Republican Party will be able to conjure a cover story to explain why they embraced a man who mocked the disabled, attacked a former POW hero, paid off a porn star from the Oval Office, defended Vladimir Putin's murder of journalists, bragged about assaulting women, and implored foreign governments to investigate his political opponents. Let's say our Republican overlords can convince us that these were just personal quirks of a "black swan" leader who kept us from the horror of . . . a former secretary of state, U.S. senator, and First Lady becoming president. To avoid the nightmare of having a president who had actually spent decades preparing for the job, it was necessary to nominate a reality-TV figure who talked openly of his desire to have sex with his own daughter and lectured Republican members of Congress on Article XII of the Constitution, which exists only in his mind. This positions Donald Trump as the Necessary Monster history demanded to save the Republican Party.

Say that combination of amnesia, self-deceit, and desperation is possible, what remains is a simple question: What does a center-right party in America stand for? Once this was easy to answer: fiscal sanity, free trade, being strong on Russia, personal responsibility, the Constitution. Now? Can anyone honestly define what the Republican Party stands for beyond "owning the libs"? Whatever that means. Can any governing party exist as a credible force with no defined principles? Can a governing party exist when the supposed Wise Men and Women of that party trampled over every value in which they swore they believed, in a desperate attempt to flee from the need to defend their values? What institution of the center right stood firm against the disgraceful idiotocracy of the Trump years? One by one the supposed leaders of the party, in office, frantically shed their uniforms of principle to don the uniform of the new ruling power. A few held firm, but in a nation that claims to value heroism under battle, the Armies of the Right fled in terror from . . . a tweet. The stench of their fear hangs over our body politic like gangrene on a rotting limb. Perhaps these men and women deserve some of our pity for their pathos, but they have proven they deserve none of our respect. They had a sworn oath to defend the country and chose to defend Donald Trump, the most anti-American president in the country's history.

On a personal level, I feel a mix of sadness and disgust. Many of these men and women lied to me when I listened to them explain why they wanted to be elected, and I and others worked so hard to get them in office and keep them in power. For what? So they could disgrace themselves by breaking every principle they swore they so deeply believed in? I blame myself for believing them, for not detecting their weakness, for helping to put them in power so that they could lie not just to me and others personally but to the nation and the world. History is a strange and unpredictable creature, but seldom is cowardice showered in glory, and I find it difficult to believe that on their deathbeds, this generation of Republicans who abandoned their allegiance to country to swear a new oath to Donald Trump will not look back on this period of their lives with a mixture of shame, sadness, and regret. Many politicians prove they stand for not very much over the course of their careers, but these men and women have proven themselves unworthy of such a benign and bland reckoning with history. This generation went out and fought and bled for . . . Donald Trump. Each bent the knee and kissed the ring, and though like the courtiers of old among them- selves they tried to convince each other they had maintained dignity and joked about the foibles of their king, they know in their hearts they have proven to be small men and women unworthy of the greatness of the country they were elected to defend.

These are not evil people. Live next door to most of them, and they will be good neighbors who help out when they can, laugh at your jokes, cheer for sports teams you both love. This was my tribe. I did not think them perfect; no man may be a hero to his valet or political consultant. I never pretended to see even glimmers of greatness in most of them, but I did hold out for an assumption of decency. They have proven me wrong, and the sadness I feel is difficult to express. No one wanted this moral test, but most of my tribe have failed it. When and if my old friends read these words, some will be angry with me and feel betrayed. They will call me hypocriti- cal for happily taking the rewards of the tribe—money, access to power, something that hints at influence—then choosing to betray my fellow members. For this charge I have no answer. They are right. I did. I ate the queen's bread and fought the queen's wars. While they worked through the tedious process of government, trying to make a difference on the edges, I left that hard work to others and spent my non-campaign time roaming the globe chasing snow, in pursuit of athletic chal- lenges with no meaning. They would argue they did the hard work and I was over-rewarded for playing a bit part in our political drama.

That's all true. But as much as they may try to blame me, I am confident I have asked myself the same and much tougher questions with the hollow realization I had no good answers. I can't change any of that. But as imperfect a messenger as I may be, what my tribe has encouraged, blessed, and promoted should not be forgotten or forgiven. Even if Donald Trump loses in 2020, the Republican Party has legitimized bigotry and hate as an organizing principle for a major political party in a country with a unique role in the world. While it is true that many of the institutions, particularly the judiciary, have survived this stress test of Trump anti-Americanism, it is despite the Republican Party, not with its encouragement and blessing. A few years ago it was possible to read a professional hate website like Breitbart and sort of chuckle that this was the odd corner of the political universe where the weirdos and freaks hung out to share grievances. Now that can be said of the national Republican Party. From the party of Lincoln, Republicans have become the party that endorsed Roy Moore and cheered when the man they would choose for president called Mexicans "rapists." The White House welcomes and empowers those on the right who peddle conspiracy theories and religious and racial bigotry on the internet. Strange, angry freaks like Sebastian Gorka and Stephen Miller are celebrated, not shunned. Across the country almost every state party is now dominated by the angry and aggrieved who seem to believe the purpose of our politics is to make America at last safe for white people.

These are the new segregationists, who have convinced

themselves they are fighting a just war to defend the values of "our way of life." They are unified by a shared vision of America not as a just force to help equalize the worst impulses of society but rather as a heavy mace they can use to club the future into submission. They will and do lie and swear they are trying to "save America," but what dark force in politics has not argued some noble purpose to justify its betrayals of decency? In today's Republican Party, a George W. Bush would be crushed by a Sean Hannity, whose growing body and seemingly enlarging head respond to lies like Pinocchio's nose. The Trump Republican Party has abandoned any pretense of kindness or compassion as a desirable human quality. All his life Donald Trump has seen these as weaknesses, not virtues worthy of aspiration. Now so it is with the Republican Party.

So how does this change? Only through defeat and desperation. Any appeal to country over party has long been proven as ineffective as a Texas governor organizing days of prayer for rain. What must be understood is that these Republicans like what they are championing. They like being the voice of white America. It is impossible to move them by any appeal to patriotism because they see themselves as putting patriotism first when they fight for their misguided vision of America. The party will only change when its desire to revel in its worst instincts is challenged by its fear of losing power. There will be a role for a white party for a long time in America, but it will soon not be a party that can win national elections, and perhaps that will force the party to adapt. But that will take a long time, and history tells us that once those in power legitimize hate, it is difficult to manage. There has always been a market for hate in America, but it's never been the dominant market. But we've never had a major party led by a man so consumed with hate and so deeply broken. There have been the Father Coughlin–like figures before, but Father Coughlin was never president. Donald Trump did not change the Republican Party as much as he gave the party permission to reveal its true self. The Lindsey Grahams of the world have not changed. We are only now seeing who they always were, freed from any need to pretend.

The Republican Party has many weapons it will use to fight to remain in power. But it seems clear that embracing change will not be among them. Even though the party has all but abandoned any pretense of a moral justification for its existence except to defeat Democrats, it remains the official party of a white governing class in America, and with that comes tremendous money and power that will be employed to defend the party. But how long can a political party that is defined as a white party cling to power in a country changing as rapidly as America? The proper perspective in contemplating the future of the Republican Party is not that of the Whigs or the Bull Moose Party but rather that of a colonial power in a foreign land. Like the Raj, unless the party changes, its future is determined, with only the question of how long until the decline becomes a rout and it collapses inward like a dying star.

Today there exist two Republican parties that are linked mostly in name only: the Republican Party of Washington elected officials and the infrastructures that support them, and the Republican governors. The dichotomy is striking. Some of these governors seem to understand their role is to govern and solve problems, not just raise money, attack Democrats, and go on Fox News. In the Northeast in deeply Democratic states, three Republican governors—Phil Scott of Vermont, Charlie Baker of Massachusetts, and Larry Hogan of Maryland—are among the most popular governors in America. They are the last outposts of a dying civilization, the socially moderate, fiscally conservative Republican Party. I've worked for all three. I'd like to say that their breed will continue, but it's difficult to understand how what they represent can coexist with the empowerment of the Trump elements within their state parties. Their greatest electoral difficulties lie not with the larger electorate but within their own party. Can their success push the Republican Party into the future? In a world in which whatever happens in Washington dominates the national conversation like never before, it's difficult to imagine the calm competence of these Republican governors having much impact on the direction of the Republican Party.

In the many campaigns I worked in, I was invariably the optimist, the guy who thought we always had a chance, that no setback couldn't be overcome. I didn't win every race, but I won most of them, and I always thought there was the possibility of winning, if only that one perfect ad or argument could be conjured. I never walked out on the field and thought we couldn't win, whatever the odds. So I find myself in a very strange and uncomfortable position of looking out at the political landscape and seeing no reason for hope that the party I spent decades working for can be redeemed. Nor any compelling reason it should be. As the Democratic Party drifts more leftward, there is an urgent need for a center-right party to argue for a different vision and governing philosophy. But how can the party that gave us Donald Trump be a legitimate voice for conservatism as a positive force? Without moral legitimacy, a center-right party becomes a soufflé of grievances and anger that exists to settle scores, not solve problems. A political party without a higher purpose is nothing more than a cartel, a syndicate. No one asks what is the greater good OPEC is trying to achieve. Its purpose is to sell oil at the highest prices possible. So it is with today's Republican Party. It is a cartel that exists to elect Republicans. There is no organized, coherent purpose other than the acquisition and maintenance of power.

Donald Trump has served a useful purpose by exposing the deep flaws of a major American political party. Like a heavy truck driven over a bridge on the edge of collapse, Trump has made it impossible to ignore the long-developing fault lines and failures of the Republican Party. A party rooted in decency and values does not embrace the vicious hate that Donald Trump peddles as patriotism. But the Republican Party did and does. This moment should signal a day of reckoning for the party and all who claim it as a political identity. Will it? I'm not hopeful. Better than most, I know the seductive lure of believing what you prefer to believe and ignoring the obvious truth.

What the Republican Party must realize is that it needs America more than America needs the party. And the America it needs is the one that is 320 million Americans and growing, a country of immigrants and less white every day: the real America, not the gauzy Shangri-La of suburban bliss that never existed. I'd like to say I believe the party I spent so many years fighting for could rise to that challenge. But that would be a lie, and there have been too many lies for too long.

ACKNOWLEDGMENTS

A special note of appreciation to Scott Merriman, who greatly assisted in sourcing and footnoting as well as bringing general smarts and a great reader's eye to the entire effort. Many thanks to Lynette Smith, who helped transform a rough first draft of misspellings and strange typos into far more readable form. Reid Singer was extraordinarily helpful in the fact-checking and research of *It Was All a Lie*. As always, all mistakes and errors are completely my fault and responsibility.

And a very heartfelt expression of gratitude to Andrew Miller, Maris Dyer, and the entire Knopf editorial team. I grew up reading Knopf authors and seeing my writing published under the Knopf name is one dream of my youth that I feel so very fortunate to have come true.

Lastly, my deepest appreciation to Peter Matson of the Sterling Lord Literistic Agency. It has been often observed that it is impossible to get published without an agent and impossible to get an agent without being published. I was somehow fortunate enough to avoid that paradox and have been guided and supported by Peter Matson from the first nutty idea I had about writing a book retracing Peter Fleming's journey across China. He is the rarest combination of encouraging but critical, a superb reader, and I have no doubt I would never have been published without his wisdom. Eight books later, he's changed my life and I will be forever grateful.

NOTES

CHAPTER 1: RACE, THE ORIGINAL REPUBLICAN SIN

1. Bob Herbert, "Impossible, Ridiculous, Repugnant," *New York Times,* Oct. 6, 2005, www.nytimes.com.
2. Theodore White, *The Making of the President, 1960* (New York: HarperPerennial, 2009).
3. Office of the Historian, "Election Statistics, 1920 to the Present," history.house.gov.
4. Roper Center, "How Groups Voted in 2012," ropercenter.cornell .edu.
5. Ian Haney López, *Dog Whistle Politics: How Coded Racial Appeals Have Reinvented Racism and Wrecked the Middle Class* (New York: Oxford University Press, 2015).
6. Seymour Martin Lipset, ed., *Emerging Coalitions in American Politics* (New Brunswick, N.J.: Transaction, 1978), 309–10.
7. Martin Schram, "A Taxing Question for Presidents," *Valley News,* May 9, 2019, www.vnews.com.
8. Steve Chapman, "The Truth About Obama and Welfare Reform," RealClearPolitics, Aug. 26, 2012, www.realclearpolitics.com.
9. Molly Ball, "What Obama Really Did to Welfare Reform," *Atlantic,* Aug. 9, 2012, www.theatlantic.com.
10. "Transcript of Ronald Reagan's 1980 Neshoba County Fair Speech," *Neshoba Democrat,* Nov. 15, 2007, neshobademocrat .com.
11. NBC Sports Bay Area Staff, "Trump to Anthem Protesters: 'Get

That Son of a B—— off the Field,'" NBC Sports, Sept. 22, 2017, www.nbcsports.com.

12. "Exit Poll Results: How Different Groups Voted in Alabama," *Washington Post,* Dec. 13, 2017, www.washingtonpost.com.

13. Wallace, quoted in "The Stand in the Schoolhouse Door (Tuscaloosa, Alabama)," Civil Rights Teaching, www.civilrightsteaching .org.

14. Jeanne Theoharis, *A More Beautiful and Terrible History: The Uses and Misuses of Civil Rights History* (Boston: Beacon Press, 2018), 47.

15. George Packer, "Dividing the Democrats," *New Yorker,* Aug. 12, 2008, www.newyorker.com.

16. *Hearings, Reports, and Prints of the Senate Select Committee on Presidential Campaign Activities,* 402.

17. Vanessa Barker, *The Politics of Imprisonment: How the Democratic Process Shapes the Way America Punishes Offenders* (New York: Oxford University Press, 2009), 66.

18. Trump, quoted in Amber Phillips, "'They're Rapists.' President Trump's Campaign Launch Speech Two Years Later, Annotated," *Washington Post,* June 16, 2017, www.washingtonpost.com.

19. U.S. Senate, *Presidential Campaign Activities of 1972, Senate Resolution 60, Watergate and Related Activities* (Washington, D.C.: Government Publishing Office, 1973), 4199—200, www .govinfo.gov.

20. Packer, "Dividing the Democrats."

21. "Growth and Opportunity Project, RNC," *Wall Street Journal,* March 18, 2013, online.wsj.com.

22. Soraya Chemaly, "Todd Akin: It's Not a War on Women, It's a War on Critical Thinking and Democracy," *HuffPost,* Oct. 20, 2012, www.huffpost.com.

23. Meghan Keneally, "Trump Shrugs Off Hitler Comparison," ABC 7, Dec. 8, 2015, abc7.com.

24. Dallas Franklin and CNN Wire, "'His Promises Are as Worthless as a Degree from Trump University': Mitt Romney Delivers

Speech on Trump," Oklahoma's News 4, March 3, 2016, kfor .com.

CHAPTER 2: FAMILY VALUES

1. Joe Heim, "Liberty University's Jerry Falwell Jr. on Trump: 'I Can't Imagine Him Doing Anything That's Not Good for the Country,'" *Richmond Times Dispatch,* Jan. 1, 2019, www .richmond.com.
2. Robert P. Jones, "White Evangelicals Can't Quit Donald Trump," *Atlantic,* April 20, 2018, www.theatlantic.com.
3. Seth Dowland, *Family Values and the Rise of the Christian Right* (Philadelphia: University of Pennsylvania Press, 2015), Kindle.
4. Heather Kerrigan, ed., *Historic Documents of 2018* (Thousand Oaks, Calif.: CQ Press, 2019), 392.
5. Robert O. Self, *All in the Family: The Realignment of American Democracy Since the 1960s* (New York: Hill and Wang, 2012), 4.
6. Ben Howe, *The Immoral Majority: Why Evangelicals Chose Political Power over Christian Values* (New York: Broadside Books, 2019), Kindle.
7. Allan J. Lichtman, *White Protestant Nation: The Rise of the American Conservative Movement* (New York: Grove Press, 2009), 321.
8. "NGTF'S Apuzzo Debates F.P.A. Advocates on Boston TV," *Bay Area Reporter* (San Francisco), Feb. 4, 1982, 8.
9. Tony Kushner, *Angels in America: A Gay Fantasia on National Themes,* rev. ed. (New York: Theatre Communications Group, 2013), 46.
10. Stephen Strang, *God and Donald Trump* (Lake Mary, Fla.: Frontline, 2017), xv.
11. Sara Jerde, "Rafael Cruz: God Sent My Son's Wife a Sign That He Should Run for President," Talking Points Memo, Feb. 22, 2016, talkingpointsmemo.com.

12. Chuck Currie, "Rick Perry Wants God to Take over Governing of Texas, America," *HuffPost,* Sept. 13, 2011, www.huffpost.com.

13. Thomas Byrne Edsall, "Is God Really Telling Rick Perry to Run for President?," *Atlantic,* Nov. 10, 2011.

14. Jessica Martinez and Gregory A. Smith, "How the Faithful Voted: A Preliminary 2016 Analysis," Pew Research Center, Nov. 9, 2016, www.pewresearch.org.

15. Peter Wehner, "Why I Can No Longer Call Myself an Evangelical Republican," *New York Times,* Dec. 9, 2017, www.nytimes .com.

16. Rick Wilson, *Everything Trump Touches Dies: A Republican Strategist Gets Real About the Worst President Ever* (New York: Free Press, 2018).

17. Michael Gerson, "The Last Temptation," *Atlantic,* April 2018.

CHAPTER 3: THE LONG CON

1. Judd Gregg, "Judd Gregg: The GOP Abandons Fiscal Responsibility," *Hill,* April 9, 2018, thehill.com.

2. Susanne Craig and Russ Buettner, "5 Takeaways from 10 Years of Trump Tax Figures," *New York Times,* May 7, 2019, www .nytimes.com.

3. "National Republican Party Platform 2016," GOP, July 18, 2016, www.gop.com.

4. "National Republican Party Platform 2012," *New York Times,* Aug. 28, 2012, archive.nytimes.com.

5. "The Debt to the Penny and Who Holds It," TreasuryDirect, accessed July 18, 2019, treasurydirect.gov.

6. Bob Woodward and Robert Costa, "Transcript: Donald Trump Interview with Bob Woodward and Robert Costa," *Washington Post,* April 2, 2016, washingtonpost.com.

7. Paul Ryan, "Transcript: Rep. Paul Ryan's Convention Speech," National Public Radio, Aug. 29, 2012, www.npr.org.

8. Steve Clemons, "GOP Presidents Have Been the Worst Contribu-

tors to the Federal Debt," *Atlantic,* Oct. 27, 2012, www.theatlantic .com.

9. Bill Clinton, "State of the Union Address," Miller Center, Jan. 27, 1998, millercenter.org.

10. *Congressional Record, 1993, Thomas; Rep. Newt Gingrich (R-GA)* (Washington, D.C.: Government Printing Office, 1993).

11. *Congressional Record, 1993, Rep. Christopher Cox (R-CA)* (Washington, D.C.: Government Printing Office).

12. Douglas Holtz-Eakin, "Which President 'Created' More Jobs?," *Wall Street Journal,* Nov. 8, 2016, wsj.com.

13. Jessica Johnson, "President Trump Calls California High-Speed Rail a 'Green Disaster,' " *Your Central Valley,* Feb. 13, 2019, www .yourcentralvalley.com; Nancy Isenson, "How California Became Donald Trump's Most Hated State," *DW,* Nov. 23, 2018.

14. John Tierney, "Which States Are Givers and Which Are Takers? And Is That Even the Correct Way to Frame the Question?," *Atlantic,* May 5, 2014, www.theatlantic.com.

15. Martin, Jonathan, "On Win Streak, Mainline G.O.P. Takes Tougher Stance Toward Tea Party," *New York Times,* May 31, 2014, www.nytimes.com.

16. Chris Cillizza, "How Thad Cochran Won," *Washington Post,* June 24, 2014, www.washingtonpost.com.

17. Jerry Hagstrom, "Farm Groups Denounce Heritage Report; EWG, UCS Praise It," *Agweek,* Sept. 9, 2016, www.agweek.com.

18. Ibid.

19. Daren Bakst, "Farm Subsidy Apologists Are Painting a Misleading Picture: Here Are the Facts," Heritage Foundation, March 7, 2017, www.heritage.org.

20. Alex Shephard, "The Farm Bill Is Everything That's Wrong with Congress," *New Republic,* May 18, 2018, newrepublic.com.

21. Tamar Haspel, "Why Do Taxpayers Subsidize Rich Farmers?," *Washington Post,* March 15, 2018, www.washingtonpost.com.

22. Doug Bandow, "Corporate Welfare Lives On and On," *American Conservative,* Aug. 29, 2018, theamericanconservative.com.

23. Ethan Baron, "Google, Tesla, Apple, Facebook Rake in Massive Subsidies: Report," *San Jose Mercury News,* July 3, 2018, mercurynews.com.

24. John Stossel, "The Super Bowl of Corporate Welfare," *Reason,* Jan. 30, 2019, reason.com.

25. Daniel Cebul, "US Remains Top Military Spender, SIPRI Reports," *Defense News,* May 2, 2018, defensenews.com.

26. Lawrence J. Korb, Laura Conley, and Alex Rothman, "A Historical Perspective on Defense Budgets," Center for American Progress, July 6, 2011, americanprogress.org.

27. James C. Capretta, "The Necessity and Impossibility of Entitlement Reform," AEI, Oct. 24, 2018, www.aei.org.

28. Paul C. Light, "Government's Most Visible Failures, 2001–2014," Brookings Institution, July 14, 2014, brookings.edu.

29. Nancy Friedman, "Word of the Week: Kinsley Gaffe," *Fritinancy,* Aug. 22, 2011, nancyfriedman.typepad.com.

30. Peter T. Kilborne, "Achievements, but Failures, Too, for Reaganomics," *New York Times,* July 1, 1983, www.nytimes.com.

31. Jennifer Burns, *Goddess of the Market: Ayn Rand and the American Right* (New York: Oxford University Press, 2011), 275.

32. George Gilder, *Wealth and Poverty: A New Edition for the Twenty-First Century* (Washington, D.C.: Regnery, 2012), Kindle.

33. Francis X. Clines, "Reagan Attacks Mondale, Vowing Veto of Tax Rises," *New York Times,* Aug. 5, 1984, www.nytimes.com.

34. Michael Wines, "The 1992 Campaign: The Ad Campaign; Clinton, Reminding Voters of a Promise," *New York Times,* Oct. 3, 1992, www.nytimes.com.

35. Becky Little, "How a Petty Snub Led to Clinton's Government Shutdown—and the Lewinsky Affair," *History,* Dec. 13, 2018, www.history.com.

36. Dylan Matthews, "Here Is Every Previous Government Shutdown, Why They Happened, and How They Ended," *Washington Post,* Sept. 25, 2013, updated Dec. 22, 2018, washingtonpost.com.

37. "2000, Bush vs. Gore," The Living Room Candidate: Presidential

Campaign Commercials 1952–2016, www.livingroomcandidate .org.

38. Robert Denton Jr., ed., *2000 Presidential Campaign: A Communication Perspective* (Santa Barbara, Calif.: Praeger, 2002), 142.

39. Bobbie Battista, "Did Last Night's Presidential Debate Change Voters' Minds?," *TalkBack Live,* CNN, Oct. 4, 2000, edition.cnn .com.

40. David Weigel, "Remembering 'Fuzzy Math,'" *Slate,* Oct. 4, 2012, slate.com.

41. Stanley Greenberg, "Winning with the Economy—or Without It," *American Prospect,* Sept. 19, 2009, prospect.org.

42. George Bush, "Full Text of Bush's Acceptance Speech," *New York Times,* Aug. 4, 2000, movies2.nytimes.com.

43. Churchill, quoted in Benjamin F. Martin, *France in 1938* (Baton Rouge: Louisiana State University Press, 2006), 219.

CHAPTER 4: CONFEDERACY OF DUNCES

1. Jindal, quoted in Steve Peoples and Ken Thomas, "Jindal: Republicans Must Stop Being the Stupid Party," RealClearPolitics, Jan. 25, 2013, www.realclearpolitics.com.

2. Davis, quoted in Juliet Eilperin, "How the West Virginia Coal Industry Changed Federal Endangered Species Policy," *Washington Post,* May 10, 2019, www.washingtonpost.com.

3. George H. Nash, *The Conservative Intellectual Movement in America Since 1945* (Wilmington, Del.: Intercollegiate Studies Institute, 2014), Kindle.

4. Timothy Noah, "William F. Buckley, RIP: Why We Should Be (Mostly) Glad We Outlived His Brand of Conservatism," *Slate,* Feb. 27, 2008, slate.com.

5. Buckley, quoted in Ron Capshaw, "'Demanding a Recount': William F. Buckley's 1965 Campaign for Mayor of New York," *Liberty Conservative,* Dec. 9, 2016.

6. Baldwin, James, *Has the American Dream Been Achieved at the*

Expense of the American Negro?: Based on the Debate Between James Baldwin and William F. Buckley. Kindle Edition.

7. James Carney, "10 Questions for William F. Buckley," *Time,* April 5, 2005, content.time.com.

8. Anthony Cody, "The Nine Most Terrifying Words in the English Language: I'm from Big Business and I'm Here to Help," *Education Week Teacher,* June 29, 2013, blogs.edweek.com.

9. Debbie Elliot, "Integrating Ole Miss: A Transformative Deadly Riot," National Public Radio, Oct. 1, 2012, www.npr.org.

10. Stuart Stevens, *The Big Enchilada: Campaign Adventures with the Cockeyed Optimists from Texas Who Won the Biggest Prize in Politics* (New York: Free Press, 2001).

11. Allison Mitchell, "Bush Draws Campaign Theme from More than 'the Heart,'" *New York Times,* June 12, 2000, nytimes.com.

12. Myron Magnet, *The Dream and the Nightmare: The Sixties' Legacy to the Underclass* (New York: Encounter Books, 2000), Kindle.

13. "Usual Weekly Earnings of Wage and Salary Workers News Release," Bureau of Labor Statistics, www.bls.gov; Donovan Hicks, "What Trump Leaves Out When He Talks About the Black Unemployment Rate," Talk Poverty, Dec. 20, 2018, talkpoverty .org; "Basic Statistics," Talk Poverty; Janelle Jones, "The Racial Wealth Gap: How African Americans Have Been Shortchanged out of the Materials to Build Wealth," Economic Policy Institute, Feb. 13, 2017, www.epi.org; Carmel Ford, "Homeownership by Race and Ethnicity," Eye on Housing, Dec. 15, 2017, eyeonhousing; Margaret Sims, "Say African American or Black, but First Acknowledge the Persistence of Structural Racism," Urban Institute, Feb. 8, 2018, www.urban.org.

14. Donald Trump (@realDonaldTrump), Twitter, May 3, 2019, 4:25 p.m., twitter.com/realdonaldtrump/status/11244549913417 93281?lang=en.

15. German Lopez, "Roy Moore: America 'Was Great at the Time When Families Were United'—Even Though We Had Slavery," *Vox,* Dec. 8, 2017, www.vox.com.

16. Josh Hawley @HawleyMo, Twitter, May 1, 2019, 3:26 a.m., twitter.com/HawleyMo/status/1123656895909302273?s=20.

17. Stuart Stevens, "Why Beto Is Bombing (and How He Can Make a Comeback)," *Bulwark,* May 30, 2019, thebulwark.com.

18. Donald Trump (@realDonaldTrump), Twitter, March 23, 2016, 8:55 p.m., twitter.com/realdonaldtrump/status/712850174838771 712?s=20.

19. William Bennett, *The Death of Outrage: Bill Clinton and the Assault on American Ideals* (New York: Free Press, 1998).

20. Bennett, quoted in Jonathan Zimmerman, "Romney Is Right to Be Appalled by Trump's Character. All of Us Should Be," *USA Today,* Jan. 5, 2019, www.usatoday.com.

21. John Hood, "What Bill Bennett Used to Understand," *National Review,* Aug. 25, 2016, www.nationalreview.com.

22. Larry O'Connor, "Bennett: #NeverTrump-ers Put Vanity Above Country; 'Terrible Case of Moral Superiority,'" *Hot Air,* Aug. 19, 2016, hotair.com.

23. William Bennett, *The Book of Virtues* (New York: Simon & Schuster, 1996), Kindle; Bennett, *Death of Outrage,* 38.

24. Trump, quoted in Ben Craw, Rex Santus, and Gabrielle Bluestone, "We're Going to Keep Updating This List Until Trump Stops Endorsing Conspiracy Theories," *Vice News,* Nov. 30, 2017, news .vice.com.

25. Russell Muirhead and Nancy L. Rosenblum, *A Lot of People Are Saying* (Princeton, N.J.: Princeton University Press, 2019), 5.

26. Donald Trump (@realDonaldTrump), Twitter, June 13, 2018, 2:56 a.m., twitter.com/realdonaldtrump/status/100683782346973 5936?lang=en.

27. Donald Trump (@realDonaldTrump), Twitter, April 2, 2019, 4:33 a.m., twitter.com/realdonaldtrump/status/111304170873080 2176?lang=en.

CHAPTER 5: MACHINERY OF DECEPTION

1. Rand, quoted in Quote Investigator: Tracing Quotations, April 30, 2015, quoteinvestigatgor.com.

2. Liz Hayes, "15 Years Ago a Federal Court Struck Down Roy Moore's Ten Commandments Display in Alabama," Americans United for Separation of Church and State, July 3, 2018, www.au .org.

3. Emily Kraft, "Ten Commandments Monument Controversy," *Encyclopedia of Alabama*, May 12, 2008, www.encyclopediaofalabama .org.

4. "Exit Poll Results: How Different Groups Voted in Alabama."

5. Jason Le Miere, "Roy Moore Met Wife Kayla When She Was a Minor and He Was 30, at a Girls' Dance Recital," *Newsweek*, Nov. 21, 2017, www.newsweek.com.

6. Ben Jacobs, "Donald Trump Appears to Back Roy Moore," *Guardian*, Nov. 21, 2017, www.theguardian.com.

7. Yochai Benkler, Robert Faris, and Hal Roberts, *Network Propaganda: Manipulation, Disinformation, and Radicalization in American Politics* (New York: Oxford University Press, 2018), 13–14.

8. "An American Original," *Vanity Fair*, Oct. 2010, www.vanityfair .com.

9. Angie Drobnic Holan, "Lie of the Year: 'If You Like Your Health Care Plan, You Can Keep It,'" PolitiFact, Dec. 12, 2013, www .politifact.com.

10. Bill Adair and Angie Drobnic Holan, "Lie of the Year 2011: 'Republicans Voted to End Medicare,'" PolitiFact, Dec. 20, 2011, www.politifact.com.

11. Nicole Hemmer, *Messengers of the Right: Conservative Media and the Transformation of American Politics* (Philadelphia: University of Pennsylvania Press, 2016), loc. 64, Kindle.

12. Nicole Hemmer, "The Conservative War on Liberal Media Has a Long History," *Atlantic*, Jan. 17, 2014, www.theatlantic.com.

13. Hemmer, *Messengers of the Right,* loc. 706, Kindle.

14. Ibid., loc. 694.

15. Ibid., loc. 456.

16. Ibid., loc. 750.

17. Ibid., loc. 840.

18. Ibid., loc. 1252.

19. Philip Kurland, review of *McCarthy and His Enemies,* by William F. Buckley Jr. and L. Brent Bozell, *University of Chicago Law Review* 21:4 (1954), 780.

20. Rick Perlstein, *Before the Storm: Barry Goldwater and the Unmaking of the American Consensus* (New York: Bold Type Books, 2001), loc. 7, Kindle.

21. Ibid., loc. 8–9.

22. E. J. Dionne Jr., *Why the Right Went Wrong: Conservatism—from Goldwater to the Tea Party and Beyond* (New York: Simon & Schuster, 2016), 41–42, Kindle.

23. Benkler, Faris, and Roberts, *Network Propaganda,* 317.

24. Max Boot, *The Corrosion of Conservatism: Why I Left the Right* (New York: Liveright, 2018), 179.

25. Markle, quoted in Mikhaila Friel, "Donald Trump Denied Calling Meghan Markle 'Nasty' and Said Reports on His Recorded Interview Are 'Fake News,'" *Insider,* June 3, 2019, www.insider.com.

26. Trump, quoted in ibid.

27. Trump, quoted in Mahita Gajanan, "'What You're Seeing . . . Is Not Happening': People Compare This Trump Quote to George Orwell," *Time,* July 24, 2018, time.com.

28. Mollie Hemingway, "Here's Why I Didn't Fall for the Russia-Trump Conspiracy," *Federalist,* April 1, 2019, thefederalist.com.

29. Robert S. Mueller, *The Mueller Report: The Final Report of the Special Counsel on Russian Interference in the 2016 Presidential Election* (Mineola, N.Y.: Dover, 2019), 4.

30. Brian Stelter, "Amash Says Many Republican Lawmakers 'Think I'm Right,' but 'They Just Won't Say It,'" CNN, May 29, 2019, cnn.com.

CHAPTER 6: WHAT ARE THEY AFRAID OF?

1. Ed Mazza, "Omarosa Manigault: 'Every Critic, Every Detractor, Will Have to Bow Down to President Trump,'" *HuffPost,* Sept. 22, 2016, www.huffpost.com.

2. William Saletan, "Cop Stoppers: How Did the NRA Become an Enemy of Law Enforcement?," *Slate,* Feb. 28, 2018, slate.com.

3. George H. W. Bush, "Letter of Resignation Sent by Bush to Rifle Association," *New York Times,* May 11, 1995, www.nytimes .com.

4. McKay Coppins, "The Man Who Broke Politics," *Atlantic,* Oct. 17, 2018, www.theatlantic.com.

5. "Trump Incorrectly Claimed to Be Swedish for Decades," *Week,* Nov. 28, 2017, theweek.com.

6. Jessica Glenza, "Trump Wrongly Claims His Father Was Born in Germany—Again," *Guardian,* April 3, 2019, www.theguardian .com.

7. "Trump Incorrectly Claimed to Be Swedish for Decades"; Chantal DaSilva, "Where Was Donald Trump's Father Born? President's Claims That Fred Trump Was Born in Germany Are Incorrect," *Newsweek,* April 3, 2019, www.newsweek.com.

8. The Atlantic (@TheAtlantic), Twitter, Oct. 15, 2018, 12:29 p.m., twitter.com/TheAtlantic/status/1051918019088265216.

9. Frances Lee, "American Politics Is More Competitive than Ever; That's Making Partisanship Worse," *Washington Post,* Jan. 9, 2014, www.washingtonpost.com.

10. Nolan McCarty, "What We Know and Don't Know About Our Polarized Politics," *Washington Post,* Jan. 8, 2014, www .washingtonpost.com.

11. Nolan McCarty, "What We Know and Do Not Know About Our Polarized Politics," in *Political Polarization in American Politics,* ed. Daniel J. Hopkins and John Sides (London: Bloomsbury Academic, 2015), www.bloomsburycollections.com.

12. "Georgia House Dispute," *Congressional Quarterly,* Jan. 21, 1966,

255, quoted in Kief Schladweiler, *African-American Involvement in the Vietnam War: CIA, FBI, and Other Government Documents,* www.aavw.org.

13. Mike Lofgren, *The Party Is Over: How Republicans Went Crazy, Democrats Became Useless, and the Middle Class Got Shafted* (New York: Penguin Books, 2013), viii.

14. Ibid., 9–10.

15. Robert G. Kaiser, *So Damn Much Money* (New York: Vintage Books, 2010), Kindle.

16. Lofgren, *Party Is Over,* 18.

17. Suryatapa Bhattacharya, "This Survey Shows How Indian Americans Plan to Vote in the U.S. Election," *Wall Street Journal,* May 27, 2016, blogs.wsj.com.

CHAPTER 7: THE ANTI-AMERICAN PATRIOTS

1. "History of Donald Trump's Political Donations," Ballotpedia, Oct. 26, 2016, ballotpedia.org; "Donald Trump Nearly Casually Remarks About Incest with His Daughter Ivanka," *The View,* ABC, March 6, 2006, available on Fusion Media Group, YouTube post, Dec. 10, 2015, www.youtube.com/watch?v=DP7yf8 -Lk80.

2. Tom McCarthy, "Comey: I Was Sure Clinton Would Win When I Reopened Email Inquiry," *Guardian,* April 13, 2018, www .theguardian.com.

3. All quotations from the Trump-Hewitt interaction are from Jesse Berney, "Trump's Terrifying Nuke Answer at the Debate Should End His Campaign but It Won't," *Rolling Stone,* Dec. 16, 2015, www.rollingstone.com.

4. Josh Rogin, "In Debate Trump's Lack of Nuclear Knowledge on Display," *Washington Post,* Sept. 28, 2016, www.washingtonpost .com.

5. "Cruz Blasts Trump as 'Pathological Liar' as Indiana Voters Head to the Polls," PBS, May 3, 2016, www.pbs.org.

6. Steven Levitsky and Daniel Ziblatt, *How Democracies Die* (New York: Crown/Archetype, 2019), loc. 3, Kindle.

7. Franz von Papen, *Memoirs of Franz von Papen* (Pickle Partners Publishing, 2015), reprint of 1953 edition, loc. 2689, Kindle.

8. Nash, *Conservative Intellectual Movement,* loc. 132, Kindle.

9. Papen, *Memoirs,* loc. 5408, Kindle.

10. Gregory Neilson, *Analysing Franz von Papen's Memoirs and His Role in the Nazi Rise to Power,* loc. 111, Kindle.

11. Publius Decius Mus [Michael Anton], "The Flight 93 Election," *Claremont Review of Books,* Sept. 5, 2016, www.claremont .org.

12. Ibid.

13. Libby Nelson, "Why We Voted for Donald Trump: David Duke Explains the White Supremacist Charlottesville Protests," *Vox,* Aug. 12, 2017, www.vox.com.

14. "A Declaration of the Immediate Causes Which Induce and Justify the Secession of the State of Mississippi from the Federal Union," Avalon Project, avalon.law.yale.edu.

15. Decius Mus, "Flight 93 Election."

16. Publius Decius Mus [Michael Anton], "Toward a Sensible, Coherent Trumpism," *Unz Review,* March 10, 2016, www.unz.com.

17. Robert B. Reich, "How Mitch McConnell Killed the Senate," *Baltimore Sun,* April 17, 2019, www.baltimoresun.com.

18. Levitsky and Ziblatt, *How Democracies Die,* loc. 3, Kindle.

19. Ibid., 21.

20. Jill Colvin, "Trump Challenges Legitimacy of Election," AP News, Oct. 15, 2016, www.apnews.com.

21. Meghan Keneally, "A Look Back at Trump Comments Perceived by Some as Encouraging Violence," ABC News, Oct. 19, 2018, abcnews.go.com.

22. Michael Calderone, "Trump Labels Media 'Enemy' Before Putin Meeting," *Politico,* July 16, 2018, www.politico.com.

23. David Leonhardt, "Trump Encourages Violence," *New York Times,* March 18, 2019, www.nytimes.com.

24. Jonathan Chait, "Trump Isn't Inciting Violence by Mistake, but on Purpose. He Just Told Us," *New York,* Nov. 5, 2018, nymag .com.

25. Levitsky and Ziblatt, *How Democracies Die,* loc. 13, Kindle.

CHAPTER 8: THE EMPIRE'S LAST STAND

1. Anthony Cilluffo and Richard Fry, "An Early Look at the 2020 Electorate," Pew Research Center, Jan. 30, 2019, www .pewsocialtrends.org.

2. Rob Griffin, Ruy Teixeira, and William H. Frey, "America's Electoral Future: Demographic Shifts and the Future of the Trump Coalition," Center for American Progress, April 19, 2018, www .brookings.edu.

3. Josh Gerstein, "D'Souza Enters Guilty Plea," *Politico,* May 20, 2014, www.politico.com.

4. Luke Ramseh, "Joe Biden Catches Flak for Recalling Work with Miss. Segregationist Sen. James O. Eastland," *Clarion Ledger,* June 19, 2019, www.clarionledger.com.

5. Anthony Walton, *Mississippi: An American Journey* (New York: Vintage, 1997), Kindle.

6. Brooks Johnson, "Blacks and the Democratic Party," Factcheck .org, April 18, 2008, www.factcheck.org.

7. Colby Itkowitz, "Candace Owens Inaccurately Calls GOP Southern Strategy a Myth," *Houston Chronicle,* April 9, 2019, www .houstonchronicle.com.

8. Rob Griffin, Ruy Teixeira, and John Halpin, "Voter Trends in 2016: A Final Analysis," Center for American Progress, Nov. 1, 2017, www.americanprogress.org.

9. U.S. District Court for the Eastern District of Wisconsin, *Frank v. Walker* (2016), FindLaw, caselaw.findlaw.com.

10. Carol Anderson, *One Person, No Vote* (London: Bloomsbury, 2018), 42.

11. Donald Trump (@realDonald Trump), Twitter, Nov. 27, 2016,

12:30 p.m., twitter.com/realdonaldtrump/status/80297294453220 9664?lang=en.

12. Anderson, *One Person, No Vote,* loc. 2, Kindle.

13. Tova Wang, *The Politics of Voter Suppression: Defending and Expanding Americans' Right to Vote* (Ithaca, N.Y.: Cornell University Press, 2012), loc. 73, Kindle.

14. Ari Berman, *Give Us the Ballot* (New York: Farrar, Straus and Giroux, 2016), loc. 15, Kindle.

15. German Lopez, "Florida Votes to Restore Ex-felon Voting Rights with Amendment 4," *Vox,* Nov. 7, 2018, www.vox.com.

16. Rebecca Onion, "Take the Impossible 'Literacy' Test Louisiana Gave Black Voters in the 1960s," *Slate,* June 28, 2013, slate.com.

17. Peter Beinart, "The Projection President," *Atlantic,* July 14, 2017, www.theatlantic.com.

18. Paul Siegel, "The Projector in Chief," *Psychology Today,* July 29, 2018, www.psychologytoday.com.

19. Anderson, *One Person, No Vote,* loc. 2, Kindle.

20. Philip Bump, "New Data Makes It Clear: Nonvoters Handed Trump the Presidency," *Washington Post,* Aug. 9, 2018, www.washingtonpost.com.

21. Jeff Mapes, "Oregon Voters Oppose Automatic Voter Registration Bill," *Oregon Live,* March 25, 2013, www.oregonlive.com.

22. Michael Grunwald, "Trump's War on California," *Politico,* Feb. 21, 2019, www.politico.com.

23. "Census of Population and Housing, 1980," U.S. Census Bureau, 1980, www.census.gov.

24. American Factfinder, "California, 2010 Demographic Profile," U.S. Census Bureau, 2010, factfinder.census.gov.

25. Ina Jaffe, "In California, 'Republican' Is Becoming a Toxic Label," National Public Radio, Nov. 16, 2012, npr.org.

26. "Prop. 187 Approved in California," *Migration News,* Dec. 1994, migration.ucdavis.edu.

27. Jim Yardley, "The 2000 Campaign: The Texas Governor; Hispanics Give Attentive Bush Mixed Reviews," *New York Times,* Aug. 27, 2000, www.nytimes.com.

CHAPTER 9: HOW DO LIES END?

1. Neal B. Freeman, "Republican in 2020, Conservative in 2024," *National Review,* July 9, 2019, www.nationalreview.com.
2. "Jewish Columnist at Conservative Conference Calls Out Trump Misconduct," Jewish Telegraphic Agency, Feb. 25, 2018, www.jta .org.
3. Adelle M. Banks, "Russell Moore Responds to Southern Baptist Detractors," *Baptist Standard,* Dec. 20, 2016, www .baptiststandard.com.
4. Jason Schwartz, "Weekly Standard, Conservative Outlet That Criticized Trump, to Shut Down," *Politico,* Dec. 14, 2018, www .politico.com.

BIBLIOGRAPHY

Adair, Bill, and Angie Drobnic Holan. "Lie of the Year 2011: 'Republicans Voted to End Medicare.'" PolitiFact, Dec. 20, 2011. www.politifact.com.

"The American Dream and the American Negro." *New York Times,* March 7, 1965. nytimes.com.

American Factfinder. "California, 2010 Demographic Profile." U.S. Census Bureau, 2010. factfinder.census.gov.

"An American Original." *Vanity Fair,* Oct. 2010. www.vanityfair.com.

Anderson, Carol. *One Person, No Vote.* London: Bloomsbury, 2018. Kindle.

Arkedis, Jim. "Harry Reid Is Right." *Atlantic,* Aug. 8, 2012. www.theatlantic.com.

Bakst, Daren. "Farm Subsidy Apologists Are Painting a Misleading Picture: Here Are the Facts." Heritage Foundation, March 7, 2017. www.heritage.org.

Ball, Molly. "What Obama Really Did to Welfare Reform." *Atlantic,* Aug. 9, 2012. www.theatlantic.com.

Bandow, Doug. "Corporate Welfare Lives On and On." *American Conservative,* Aug. 29, 2018. theamericanconservative.com.

Banks, Adelle M. "Russell Moore Responds to Southern Baptist Detractors." *Baptist Standard,* Dec. 20, 2016. www.baptiststandard.com.

Barker, Vanessa. *The Politics of Imprisonment: How the Democratic Process Shapes the Way America Punishes Offenders.* New York: Oxford University Press, 2009.

Baron, Ethan. "Google, Tesla, Apple, Facebook Rake in Massive Subsidies: Report." *San Jose Mercury News,* July 3, 2018. mercurynews.com.

"Basic Statistics." Talk Poverty. talkpoverty.org.

Battista, Bobbie. "Did Last Night's Presidential Debate Change Voters' Minds?" *TalkBack Live.* CNN, Oct. 4, 2000. edition.cnn.com.

Beinart, Peter. "The Projection President." *Atlantic,* July 14, 2017. www.theatlantic.com.

Benkler, Yochai, Robert Faris, and Hal Roberts. *Network Propaganda: Manipulation, Disinformation, and Radicalization in American Politics.* New York: Oxford University Press, 2018.

Bennett, William. *The Book of Virtues.* New York: Simon & Schuster, 1996.

———. *The Death of Outrage: Bill Clinton and the Assault on American Ideals.* New York: Free Press, 1998.

Berman, Ari. *Give Us the Ballot.* New York: Farrar, Straus and Giroux, 2016. Kindle.

Berney, Jesse. "Trump's Terrifying Nuke Answer at the Debate Should End His Campaign but It Won't." *Rolling Stone,* Dec. 16, 2015. www.rollingstone.com.

Bhattacharya, Suryatapa. "This Survey Shows How Indian Americans Plan to Vote in the U.S. Election." *Wall Street Journal,* May 27, 2016. blogs.wsj.com.

Boot, Max. *The Corrosion of Conservatism: Why I Left the Right.* New York: Liveright, 2018. archives.gcah.org.

Buckley, William F. *The Unmaking of a Mayor.* New York: Encounter Books, 2015.

Bump, Philip. "New Data Makes It Clear: Nonvoters Handed Trump the Presidency." *Washington Post,* Aug. 9, 2018. www.washingtonpost.com.

Burns, Jennifer. *Goddess of the Market: Ayn Rand and the American Right.* New York: Oxford University Press, 2011.

Bush, George H. W. "Letter of Resignation Sent by Bush to Rifle Association." *New York Times,* May 11, 1995. www.nytimes.com.

Bush, George W. "Full Text of Bush's Acceptance Speech." *New York Times,* Aug. 4, 2000. movies2.nytimes.com.

Calderone, Michael. "Trump Labels Media 'Enemy' Before Putin Meeting." *Politico,* July 16, 2018. www.politico.com.

Capretta, James C. "The Necessity and Impossibility of Entitlement Reform." AEI, Oct. 24, 2018. www.aei.org.

Capshaw, Ron. "'Demanding a Recount': William F. Buckley's 1965 Campaign for Mayor of New York." *Liberty Conservative,* Dec. 9, 2016.

Carney, James. "10 Questions for William F. Buckley." *Time,* April 5, 2005. content.time.com.

Cebul, Daniel. "US Remains Top Military Spender, SIPRI Reports." *Defense News,* May 2, 2018. defensenews.com.

"Census of Population and Housing, 1980." U.S. Census Bureau, 1980. www.census.gov.

Chait, Jonathan. "Trump Isn't Inciting Violence by Mistake, but on Purpose. He Just Told Us." *New York,* Nov. 5, 2018. nymag.com.

Chapman, Steve. "The Truth About Obama and Welfare Reform." RealClearPolitics, Aug. 26, 2012. realclearpolitics.com.

Chemaly, Soraya. "Todd Akin: It's Not a War on Women, It's a War on Critical Thinking and Democracy." *HuffPost,* Oct. 20, 2012. www .huffpost.com.

Cillizza, Chris. "How Thad Cochran Won." *Washington Post,* June 24, 2014. www.washingtonpost.com.

Cilluffo, Anthony, and Richard Fry. "An Early Look at the 2020 Electorate." Pew Research Center, Jan. 30, 2019. www.pewsocialtrends .org.

Clemons, Steve. "GOP Presidents Have Been the Worst Contributors to the Federal Debt." *Atlantic,* Oct. 27, 2012. www.theatlantic.com.

Clines, Francis X. "Reagan Attacks Mondale, Vowing Veto of Tax Rises." *New York Times,* Aug. 5, 1984. www.nytimes.com.

Clinton, Bill. "State of the Union Address." Miller Center, Jan. 27, 1998. millercenter.org.

Cody, Anthony. "The Nine Most Terrifying Words in the English

Language: I'm from Big Business and I'm Here to Help." *Education Week Teacher,* June 29, 2013. blogs.edweek.com.

Colvin, Jill. "Trump Challenges Legitimacy of Election." AP News, Oct. 15, 2016. www.apnews.com.

Congressional Record, 1993. Rep. Christopher Cox (R-CA). Washington, D.C.: Government Printing Office, May, 27, 1993.

Congressional Record, 1993. Thomas; Rep. Newt Gingrich (R-GA). Washington, D.C.: Government Printing Office, Feb. 2, 1993.

Congressional Record: Proceedings and Debates, 119, Part 31, 40663.

Coppins, McKay. "The Man Who Broke Politics." *Atlantic,* Oct. 17, 2018. www.theatlantic.com.

Craig, Susanne, and Russ Buettner. "5 Takeaways from 10 Years of Trump Tax Figures." *New York Times,* May 7, 2019. www.nytimes.com.

Craw, Ben, Rex Santus, and Gabrielle Bluestone. "We're Going to Keep Updating This List Until Trump Stops Endorsing Conspiracy Theories." *Vice News,* Nov. 30, 2017. news.vice.com.

"Cruz Blasts Trump as 'Pathological Liar' as Indiana Voters Head to the Polls." PBS, May 3, 2016. www.pbs.org.

Currie, Chuck. "Rick Perry Wants God to Take over Governing of Texas, America." *HuffPost,* Sept. 13, 2011. www.huffpost.com.

DaSilva, Chantal. "Where Was Donald Trump's Father Born? President's Claims That Fred Trump Was Born in Germany Are Incorrect." *Newsweek,* April 3, 2019. www.newsweek.com.

Davis, Susan. "Senate Pulls 'Nuclear' Trigger to Ease Gorsuch Confirmation." National Public Radio, April 6, 2017. npr.org.

"The Debt to the Penny and Who Holds It." TreasuryDirect, accessed July 18, 2019. treasurydirect.gov.

Decius Mus, Publius [Michael Anton]. "The Flight 93 Election." *Claremont Review of Books,* Sept. 5, 2016. www.claremont.org.

———. "Toward a Sensible, Coherent Trumpism." *Unz Review,* March 10, 2016. www.unz.com.

"A Declaration of the Immediate Causes Which Induce and Justify the Secession of the State of Mississippi from the Federal Union." Avalon Project. avalon.law.yale.edu.

Denton, Robert, Jr., ed. *2000 Presidential Campaign: A Communication Perspective.* Santa Barbara, Calif.: Praeger, 2002.

Dionne, E. J. *Why the Right Went Wrong: Conservatism—from Goldwater to the Tea Party and Beyond.* New York: Simon & Schuster, 2016. Kindle.

Dowland, Seth. *Family Values and the Rise of the Christian Right.* Philadelphia: University of Pennsylvania Press, 2015. Kindle.

Drobnic Holan, Angie. "Lie of the Year: 'If You Like Your Health Care Plan, You Can Keep It.'" PolitiFact, Dec. 12, 2013. www.politifact .com.

Edsall, Thomas Byrne. "Is God Really Telling Rick Perry to Run for President?" *Atlantic,* Nov. 10, 2011.

Eilperin, Juliet. "How the West Virginia Coal Industry Changed Federal Endangered Species Policy." *Washington Post,* May 10, 2019. www.washingtonpost.com.

Elliot, Debbie. "Integrating Ole Miss: A Transformative Deadly Riot." National Public Radio, Oct. 1, 2012. www.npr.org.

"Exit Poll Results: How Different Groups Voted in Alabama." *Washington Post,* Dec. 13, 2017. www.washingtonpost.com.

Faulk, Kent. "A Roy Moore Timeline." Al.com, June 20, 2019. www .al.com.

Ford, Carmel. "Homeownership by Race and Ethnicity." Eye on Housing, Dec. 15, 2017. eyeonhousing.

Franklin, Dallas, and CNN Wire. "'His Promises Are as Worthless as a Degree from Trump University': Mitt Romney Delivers Speech on Trump." Oklahoma's News 4, March 3, 2016. kfor.com.

Freeman, Neal B. "Republican in 2020, Conservative in 2024." *National Review,* July 9, 2019. www.nationalreview.com.

Friedman, Nancy. "Word of the Week: Kinsley Gaffe." *Fritinancy,* Aug. 22, 2011. nancyfriedman.typepad.com.

Friel, Mikhaila. "Donald Trump Denied Calling Meghan Markle 'Nasty' and Said Reports on His Recorded Interview Are 'Fake News.'" *Insider,* June 3, 2019. www.insider.com.

Gajanan, Mahita. "'What You're Seeing . . . Is Not Happening':

People Compare This Trump Quote to George Orwell." *Time,* July 24, 2018. time.com.

———. "Why Republicans Are Suddenly Thanking Harry Reid for a 2013 Tweet About Filibuster Reform." *Time,* June 28, 2018. time .com.

Gerson, Michael. "The Last Temptation." *Atlantic,* April 2018.

Gerstein, Josh. "D'Souza Enters Guilty Plea." *Politico,* May 20, 2014. www.politico.com.

Gilder, George. *Wealth and Poverty: A New Edition for the Twenty-First Century.* Washington, D.C.: Regnery, 2012. Kindle.

Glenza, Jessica. "Trump Wrongly Claims His Father Was Born in Germany—Again." *Guardian,* April 3, 2019. www.theguardian.com.

Greenberg, Stanley. "Winning with the Economy—or Without It." *American Prospect,* Sept. 19, 2009. prospect.org.

Gregg, Judd. "Judd Gregg: The GOP Abandons Fiscal Responsibility." *Hill,* April 9, 2018. thehill.com.

Griffin, Rob, Ruy Teixeira, and William H. Frey. "America's Electoral Future: Demographic Shifts and the Future of the Trump Coalition." Center for American Progress, April 19, 2018. www .brookings.edu.

Griffin, Rob, Ruy Teixeira, and John Halpin. "Voter Trends in 2016: A Final Analysis." Center for American Progress, Nov. 1, 2017. www .americanprogress.org.

"Growth and Opportunity Project, RNC." *Wall Street Journal,* March 18, 2013. online.wsj.com.

Grunwald, Michael. "Trump's War on California." *Politico,* Feb. 21, 2019. www.politico.com.

Hagstrom, Jerry. "Farm Groups Denounce Heritage Report; EWG, UCS Praise It." *Agweek,* Sept. 9, 2016. www.agweek.com.

Haney López, Ian. *Dog Whistle Politics: How Coded Racial Appeals Have Reinvented Racism and Wrecked the Middle Class.* New York: Oxford University Press, 2015.

Haspel, Tamar. "Why Do Taxpayers Subsidize Rich Farmers?" *Washington Post,* March 15, 2018. www.washingtonpost.com.

Hayes, Liz. "15 Years Ago a Federal Court Struck Down Roy Moore's Ten Commandments Display in Alabama." Americans United for Separation of Church and State, July 3, 2018. www.au.org.

Hearings, Reports, and Prints of the Senate Select Committee on Presidential Campaign Activities. Washington, D.C.: Government Printing Office, 1973.

Heim, Joe. "Liberty University's Jerry Falwell Jr. on Trump: 'I Can't Imagine Him Doing Anything That's Not Good for the Country.'" *Richmond Times Dispatch,* Jan. 1, 2019. www.richmond.com.

Hemingway, Mollie. "Here's Why I Didn't Fall for the Russia-Trump Conspiracy." *Federalist,* April 1, 2019. thefederalist.com.

Hemmer, Nicole. "The Conservative War on Liberal Media Has a Long History." *Atlantic,* Jan. 17, 2014. www.theatlantic.com.

————. *Messengers of the Right: Conservative Media and the Transformation of American Politics.* Philadelphia: University of Pennsylvania Press, 2016. Kindle.

Herbert, Bob. "Impossible, Ridiculous, Repugnant." *New York Times,* Oct. 6, 2005. www.nytimes.com.

Hicks, Donovan. "What Trump Leaves Out When He Talks About the Black Unemployment Rate." Talk Poverty, Dec. 20, 2018. talkpoverty.org.

"History of Donald Trump's Political Donations." Ballotpedia, Oct. 26, 2016. ballotpedia.org.

Holtz-Eakin, Douglas. "Which President 'Created' More Jobs?" *Wall Street Journal,* Nov. 8, 2016. wsj.com.

Homans, Charles. "Mitch McConnell Got Everything He Wanted. But at What Cost?" *New York Times,* Jan. 22, 2019. www.nytimes.com.

Hood, John. "What Bill Bennett Used to Understand." *National Review,* Aug. 25, 2016. www.nationalreview.com.

Howe, Ben. *The Immoral Majority: Why Evangelicals Chose Political Power over Christian Values.* New York: Broadside Books, 2019. Kindle.

Isenson, Nancy. "How California Became Donald Trump's Most Hated State." *DW,* Nov. 23, 2018.

Itkowitz, Colby. "Candace Owens Inaccurately Calls GOP Southern Strategy a Myth." *Houston Chronicle,* April 9, 2019. www.houstonchronicle.com.

Jacobs, Ben. "Donald Trump Appears to Back Roy Moore." *Guardian,* Nov. 21, 2017. www.theguardian.com.

Jaffe, Ina. "In California, 'Republican' Is Becoming a Toxic Label." National Public Radio, Nov. 16, 2012. npr.org.

Jerde, Sara. "Rafael Cruz: God Sent My Son's Wife a Sign That He Should Run for President." Talking Points Memo, Feb. 22, 2016. talkingpointsmemo.com.

"Jewish Columnist at Conservative Conference Calls Out Trump Misconduct." Jewish Telegraphic Agency, Feb. 25, 2018. www.jta.org.

Johnson, Brooks. "Blacks and the Democratic Party." Factcheck.org, April 18, 2008. www.factcheck.org.

Johnson, Jessica. "President Trump Calls California High-Speed Rail a 'Green Disaster.'" *Your Central Valley,* Feb. 13, 2019. www.yourcentralvalley.com.

Jones, Janelle. "The Racial Wealth Gap: How African Americans Have Been Shortchanged out of the Materials to Build Wealth." Economic Policy Institute, Feb. 13, 2017. www.epi.org.

Jones, Robert P. "White Evangelicals Can't Quit Donald Trump." *Atlantic,* April 20, 2018. www.theatlantic.com.

Kaiser, Robert G. *So Damn Much Money.* New York: Vintage Books, 2010. Kindle.

Keneally, Meghan. "A Look Back at Trump Comments Perceived by Some as Encouraging Violence." ABC News, Oct. 19, 2018. abcnews.go.com.

———. "Trump Shrugs Off Hitler Comparison." ABC 7, Dec. 8, 2015. abc7.com.

Kerrigan, Heather, ed. *Historic Documents of 2018.* Thousand Oaks, Calif.: CQ Press, 2019.

Kilborne, Peter T. "Achievements, but Failures, Too, for Reaganomics." *New York Times,* July 1, 1983. www.nytimes.com.

The Klan Manual. Center for History and New Media. chnm.gmu.edu.

Korb, Lawrence J., Laura Conley, and Alex Rothman. "A Historical Perspective on Defense Budgets." Center for American Progress, July 6, 2011. americanprogress.org.

Kraft, Emily. "Ten Commandments Monument Controversy." *Encyclopedia of Alabama,* May 12, 2008. www.encyclopediaofalabama .org/article/h-1525.

Krogstad, Jens Manuel, Antonio Flores, and Mark Hugo Lopez. "Key Takeaways About Latino Voters in the 2018 Midterm Elections." Pew Research Center, Nov. 9, 2018. www.pewresearch.org.

Kurland, Philip. Review of *McCarthy and His Enemies,* by William F. Buckley Jr. and L. Brent Bozell. 21 *University of Chicago Law Review* 780 (1954). chicagounbound.uchicago.edu.

Kushner, Tony. *Angels in America: A Gay Fantasia on National Themes.* Rev. ed. New York: Theatre Communications Group, 2013.

Lee, Frances. "American Politics Is More Competitive Than Ever; That's Making Partisanship Worse." *Washington Post,* Jan. 9, 2014. www.washingtonpost.com.

Le Miere, Jason. "Roy Moore Met Wife Kayla When She Was a Minor and He Was 30, at a Girls' Dance Recital." *Newsweek,* Nov. 21, 2017. www.newsweek.com.

Leonhardt, David. "Trump Encourages Violence." *New York Times,* March 18, 2019. www.nytimes.com.

Levitsky, Steven, and Daniel Ziblatt. *How Democracies Die.* New York: Crown/Archetype, 2019. Kindle.

Lichtman, Allan J. *White Protestant Nation: The Rise of the American Conservative Movement.* New York: Grove Press, 2009.

Light, Paul C. "Government's Most Visible Failures, 2001–2014." Brookings Institution, July 14, 2014. brookings.edu.

Lipset, Seymour Martin, ed. *Emerging Coalitions in American Politics.* New Brunswick, N.J.: Transaction, 1978.

Little, Becky. "How a Petty Snub Led to Clinton's Government Shutdown—and the Lewinsky Affair." *History,* Dec. 13, 2018. www .history.com.

Lofgren, Mike. *The Party Is Over: How Republicans Went Crazy,*

Democrats Became Useless, and the Middle Class Got Shafted. New York: Penguin Books, 2013.

Lopez, German. "Florida Votes to Restore Ex-felon Voting Rights with Amendment 4." *Vox,* Nov. 7, 2018. www.vox.com.

———. "Roy Moore: America 'Was Great at the Time When Families Were United'—Even Though We Had Slavery." *Vox,* Dec. 8, 2017. www.vox.com.

Magnet, Myron. *The Dream and the Nightmare: The Sixties' Legacy to the Underclass.* New York: Encounter Books, 2000. Kindle.

Mapes, Jeff. "Oregon Voters Oppose Automatic Voter Registration Bill." *Oregon Live,* March 25, 2013. www.oregonlive.com.

Martin, Benjamin F. *France in 1938.* Baton Rouge: Louisiana State University Press, 2006.

Martinez, Jessica, and Gregory A. Smith. "How the Faithful Voted: A Preliminary 2016 Analysis." Pew Research Center, Nov. 9, 2016. www.pewresearch.org.

Matthews, Dylan. "Here Is Every Previous Government Shutdown, Why They Happened, and How They Ended." *Washington Post,* Sept. 25, 2013, updated Dec. 22, 2018. washingtonpost.com.

Mazza, Ed. "Omarosa Manigault: 'Every Critic, Every Detractor, Will Have to Bow Down to President Trump.'" *HuffPost,* Sept. 22, 2016. www.huffpost.com.

McCarthy, Tom. "Comey: I Was Sure Clinton Would Win When I Reopened Email Inquiry." *Guardian,* April 13, 2018. www.theguardian.com.

McCarty, Nolan. "What We Know and Do Not Know About Our Polarized Politics." In *Political Polarization in American Politics,* edited by Daniel J. Hopkins and John Sides. London: Bloomsbury Academic, 2015. www.bloomsburycollections.com.

———. "What We Know and Don't Know About Our Polarized Politics." *Washington Post,* Jan. 8, 2014. www.washingtonpost.com.

Mitchell, Allison. "Bush Draws Campaign Theme from More than 'the Heart.'" *New York Times,* June 12, 2000. nytimes.com.

Mueller, Robert S. *The Mueller Report: The Final Report of the Special Counsel on Russian Interference in the 2016 Presidential Election.* Mineola, N.Y.: Dover, 2019.

Muirhead, Russell, and Nancy L. Rosenblum. *A Lot of People Are Saying.* Princeton, N.J.: Princeton University Press, 2019.

Nash, George H. *The Conservative Intellectual Movement in America Since 1945.* Wilmington, Del.: Intercollegiate Studies Institute, 2014. Kindle.

"National Republican Party Platform 2012." *New York Times,* Aug. 28, 2012. archive.nytimes.com.

"National Republican Party Platform 2016." GOP, July 18, 2016. www .gop.com.

NBC Sports Bay Area Staff. "Trump to Anthem Protesters: 'Get That Son of a B—— off the Field.'" NBC Sports, Sept. 22, 2017. www .nbcsports.com.

Neilson, Gregory. *Analysing Franz von Papen's Memoirs and His Role in the Nazi Rise to Power.* Kindle.

Nelson, Libby. "Why We Voted for Donald Trump: David Duke Explains the White Supremacist Charlottesville Protests." *Vox,* Aug. 12, 2017. www.vox.com.

"NGTF'S Apuzzo Debates F.P.A. Advocates on Boston TV." *Bay Area Reporter* (San Francisco), Feb. 4, 1982.

Noah, Timothy. "William F. Buckley, RIP: Why We Should Be (Mostly) Glad We Outlived His Brand of Conservatism." *Slate,* Feb. 27, 2008. slate.com.

O'Connor, Larry. "Bennett: #NeverTrump-ers Put Vanity Above Country; 'Terrible Case of Moral Superiority.'" *Hot Air,* Aug. 19, 2016. hotair.com.

Office of the Historian. "Election Statistics, 1920 to the Present." House of Representatives, history.house.gov.

Onion, Rebecca. "Take the Impossible 'Literacy' Test Louisiana Gave Black Voters in the 1960s." *Slate,* June 28, 2013. slate.com.

Packer, George. "Dividing the Democrats." *New Yorker,* Aug. 12, 2008. www.newyorker.com.

Papen, Franz von. *Memoirs of Franz von Papen.* Pickle Partners Publishing, 2015. Kindle. Reprint of 1953 edition.

Peoples, Steve, and Ken Thomas. "Jindal: Republicans Must Stop Being the Stupid Party." RealClearPolitics, Jan. 25, 2013. www.realclearpolitics.com.

Perlstein, Rick. *Before the Storm: Barry Goldwater and the Unmaking of the American Consensus.* New York: Bold Type Books, 2001. Kindle.

Phillips, Amber. " 'They're Rapists.' President Trump's Campaign Launch Speech Two Years Later, Annotated." *Washington Post,* June 16, 2017. www.washingtonpost.com.

"Prop. 187 Approved in California." *Migration News,* Dec. 1994. migration.ucdavis.edu.

Ramseh, Luke. "Joe Biden Catches Flak for Recalling Work with Miss. Segregationist Sen. James O. Eastland." *Clarion Ledger,* June 19, 2019. www.clarionledger.com.

Reagan, Ronald. "A Time for Choosing Speech, 1964." Fordham University. legacy.fordham.edu.

Reich, Robert B. "How Mitch McConnell Killed the Senate." *Baltimore Sun,* April 17, 2019. www.baltimoresun.com.

Rogin, Josh. "In Debate Trump's Lack of Nuclear Knowledge on Display." *Washington Post,* Sept. 28, 2016. www.washingtonpost.com.

Roper Center. "How Groups Voted in 2012." ropercenter.cornell.edu.
———. "How Groups Voted in 2016." ropercenter.cornell.edu.
———. "How Groups Voted in 2019." ropercenter.cornell.edu.

Ryan, Paul. "Transcript: Rep. Paul Ryan's Convention Speech." National Public Radio, Aug. 29, 2012. www.npr.org.

Saletan, William. "Cop Stoppers: How Did the NRA Become an Enemy of Law Enforcement?" *Slate,* Feb. 28, 2018. slate.com.

Schladweiler, Kief. *African-American Involvement in the Vietnam War: CIA, FBI, and Other Government Documents.* www.aavw.org.

Schram, Martin. "A Taxing Question for Presidents." *Valley News,* May 9, 2019. www.vnews.com.

Schwartz, Jason. "Weekly Standard, Conservative Outlet That Criticized Trump, to Shut Down." *Politico,* Dec. 14, 2018. www.politico .com.

Scott, Eugene. "Six Times President Trump Said He Is the Least Racist Person." *Washington Post,* Jan. 17, 2018. www.washingtonpost .com.

Self, Robert O. *All in the Family: The Realignment of American Democracy Since the 1960s.* New York: Hill and Wang, 2012.

Shephard, Alex. "The Farm Bill Is Everything That's Wrong with Congress." *New Republic,* May 18, 2018. newrepublic.com.

Siegel, Paul. "The Projector in Chief." *Psychology Today,* July 29, 2018. www.psychologytoday.com.

Sims, Margaret. "Say African American or Black, but First Acknowledge the Persistence of Structural Racism." Urban Institute, Feb. 8, 2018. www.urban.org.

"The Stand in the Schoolhouse Door (Tuscaloosa, Alabama)." Civil Rights Teaching. www.civilrightsteaching.org.

Stelter, Brian. "Amash Says Many Republican Lawmakers 'Think I'm Right,' but 'They Just Won't Say It.'" CNN, May 29, 2019. cnn.com.

Stevens, Stuart. *The Big Enchilada: Campaign Adventures with the Cockeyed Optimists from Texas Who Won the Biggest Prize in Politics.* New York: Free Press, 2001.

———. *Scorched Earth: A Political Love Story.* New York: Atlantic Monthly Press, 1994.

———. "Why Beto Is Bombing (and How He Can Make a Comeback)." *Bulwark,* May 30, 2019. thebulwark.com.

St. John, Warren. "A Republican Renaissance Man." Talk of the Town. *New Yorker,* Nov. 27, 1994. www.newyorker.com.

Stossel, John. "The Super Bowl of Corporate Welfare." *Reason,* Jan. 30, 2019. reason.com.

Strang, Stephen. *God and Donald Trump.* Lake Mary, Fla.: Frontline, 2017.

Theoharis, Jeanne. *A More Beautiful and Terrible History: The Uses and Misuses of Civil Rights History.* Boston: Beacon Press, 2018.

Tierney, John. "Which States Are Givers and Which Are Takers? And Is That Even the Correct Way to Frame the Question?" *Atlantic,* May 5, 2014. www.theatlantic.com.

"Transcript of Ronald Reagan's 1980 Neshoba County Fair Speech." *Neshoba Democrat,* Nov. 15, 2007. neshobademocrat.com.

"Trump Incorrectly Claimed to Be Swedish for Decades." *Week,* Nov. 28, 2017. theweek.com.

"2000, Bush vs. Gore." The Living Room Candidate: Presidential Campaign Commercials 1952–2016. www.livingroomcandidate .org.

U.S. District Court for the Eastern District of Wisconsin. *Frank v. Walker* (2016). FindLaw. caselaw.findlaw.com.

U.S. Senate. *Presidential Campaign Activities of 1972, Senate Resolution 60, Watergate and Related Activities.* Washington, D.C.: Government Publishing Office, 1973. www.govinfo.gov.

"Usual Weekly Earnings of Wage and Salary Workers News Release." Bureau of Labor Statistics. www.bls.gov.

Wallace, George. "Speech at Serb Hall, 1976." University of Maryland. umd.edu.

Walton, Anthony. *Mississippi: An American Journey.* New York: Vintage, 1997. Kindle.

Wang, Tova. *The Politics of Voter Suppression: Defending and Expanding Americans' Right to Vote.* Ithaca, N.Y.: Cornell University Press, 2012. Kindle.

Wehner, Peter. "Why I Can No Longer Call Myself an Evangelical Republican." *New York Times,* Dec. 9, 2017. www.nytimes.com.

Weigel, David. "Remembering 'Fuzzy Math.'" *Slate,* Oct. 4, 2012. slate.com.

White, Theodore. *The Making of the President, 1960.* New York: HarperPerennial, 2009.

Wilson, Rick. *Everything Trump Touches Dies: A Republican Strategist Gets Real About the Worst President Ever.* New York: Free Press, 2018.

Wines, Michael. "The 1992 Campaign: The Ad Campaign; Clinton,

Reminding Voters of a Promise." *New York Times,* Oct. 3, 1992. www.nytimes.com.

Woodward, Bob, and Robert Costa. "Transcript: Donald Trump Interview with Bob Woodward and Robert Costa." *Washington Post,* April 2, 2016. washingtonpost.com.

Yardley, Jim. "The 2000 Campaign: The Texas Governor; Hispanics Give Attentive Bush Mixed Reviews." *New York Times,* Aug. 27, 2000. www.nytimes.com.

Zimmerman, Jonathan. "Romney Is Right to Be Appalled by Trump's Character. All of Us Should Be." *USA Today,* Jan. 5, 2019. www.usatoday.com.

A NOTE ABOUT THE AUTHOR

Stuart Stevens is the author of seven previous books, and his work has appeared in *The New York Times, The Washington Post, Esquire,* and *Outside,* among other publications. He has written extensively for television shows, including *Northern Exposure, Commander in Chief,* and *K Street.* For twenty-five years, he was the lead strategist and media consultant for some of the nation's toughest political campaigns. He attended Colorado College; Pembroke College, Oxford; Middlebury College; and UCLA film school. He is a former fellow of the American Film Institute.

A NOTE ON THE TYPE

The text of this book was set in Sabon, a typeface designed by Jan Tschichold (1902–1974).

Typeset by Scribe,
Philadelphia, Pennsylvania

Printed and bound by LSC Communications,
Harrisonburg, Virginia

Designed by Michael Collica